Dominic Di Benedetto J. M. J+

THE LAYMAN IN THE CHURCH

THE LAYMAN IN
THE CHURCH

by

MICHAEL DE LA BEDOYERE

HENRY REGNERY COMPANY
CHICAGO, 1955

NIHIL OBSTAT : RICCARDVS ROCHE, S.T.D.
CENSOR DEPVTATVS
IMPRIMATVR : LAURENTIVS P. EMERY
VICARIVS GENERALIS
BIRMINGAMIAE : DIE XVIII AVGVSTI MCMLIV

PRINTED IN GREAT BRITAIN

CONTENTS

INTRODUCTION

THESE pages could not have been written in their present form but for Père Congar's great work *Jalons pour une Théologie du Laïcat*, published recently. Not being a theologian, I owe to him the central scheme on which my argument is based, namely the participation of every Catholic in the priestly, prophetical and regal functions of Christ. But Père Congar's 680 learned pages are not for the average layman, nor, I imagine, for many a busy priest. Nor am I capable of summarizing or reporting another person's work. What I read leads me, willy nilly, to speculate for myself. Hence I have tried, in a short book and in reasonably popular language, to work out for myself certain points which seem to be implied in that Theology of the Laity.

Both in self-defence and in defence of Père Congar, I must also add that those who have read my previous book, *Living Christianity*, will recognize in this one the same fundamental position. That book was written long before I had read any of Père Congar's writings. So, while expressing my great debt to the Dominican theologian for giving me a far more solid basis for ideas and views which I have been trying to work out for some time, no one must suppose that he bears the slightest responsibility for what is to be found here.

M. B.

I

THE CHURCH APART

"IT is a remarkable characteristic of the nineteenth century that it witnessed a widening of the gulf between priest and layman, more especially in an emotional sense", wrote the late Dr. Paul Simon in *The Human Element in the Church of Christ*. Explaining why this gulf arose, this German priest-professor showed how it was closely linked "with the secular bourgeois spirit, fathered by the French Revolution, although other spiritual influences may have played a part". In the "progressive secularization of every branch of life" which has resulted from the new ideas,

> the Church found itself in a very peculiar position. Even amongst the multitudes of the faithful the Church was a thing apart having nothing to do with the rest of life (it was like a Sunday amongst the days of the week). The Church should be left alone; but on the condition that it did not disturb any other fields of life. It is a matter for the clergy, it was said, who while performing certain functions for the people do not belong to the people. Is it not in reality a Church for priests? Do they not unite in themselves all the ecclesiastical functions? Is it not they who take the sole initiative when new ecclesiastical tasks crop up? Is not the education of the priest such as to make him a man apart? What voice does the laity possess in the Church?[1]

A century and a half after the French Revolution, the Church of France was faced with the virtual paganization of the whole country with the exception of a minority whose religious life was closely associated with clericalism, as clericalism was too often associated with the politics of conservatism. This situation, despite many efforts to overcome it, had set up, in the words of a Cardinal Archbishop of Paris, "a wall between the Church and the people". In order to begin the work of breaking

[1] *The Human Element in the Church of Christ* by the Rev. Dr. Paul Simon, pp. 83, 84 (Mercier Press).

down that wall where it was toughest, the mission of the priest-worker was started.

On reflection, one begins to realize how very extraordinary this conception was. In certain peasant countries suddenly acquiring democratic constitutions, it was often necessary for the priest to enter politics in order to protect the interests of the otherwise leaderless Catholics. But the necessity was bound to reflect on the failure to educate the Catholic people to wider Christian responsibilities, and no one would suggest that the rôle of priest-politician made a good mixture, either in the interests of the Church or of the State. What of the priest-worker? The idea appealed because it enabled the priest to share the exploitation and the poverty of the people, but the full implications of the point that the priest would also have to share the conditions of factory work and the political commitments of the people was overlooked. Without doubt, the priest-worker, like the priest-soldier, the priest in internment camps, the priest in certain foreign missionary conditions, has been given the opportunity of a life of self-dedication that has magnificently reflected Christlike qualities and effected immense apostolic good. He, too, has learnt—learnt at times too well—how separate from the people the sacerdotal life has become. But the experiment had to fail in the end—valuable as the failure was—because it derived from the long-standing separation of Church from people the causes of which go much deeper than the visible hostility between clericalism and anti-clericalism in a country like France. For all its courage, it was an attempt to repair a breach by trying to patch it at its widest point instead of working from where the foundations were sound and making the whole good.

Dr. Simon, in emphasizing the long-standing "clericalism" of the Church itself, put his finger on the basic cause of the wall that separates the Church from the world, though it must be pointed out that the historical causes of this "clericalism" are extremely complex and by no means the sole responsibility of churchmen. This wall does not only separate the Church from the hostile paganized masses in once Catholic countries. It exists in all countries, and it even exists within the Church itself. In both Catholic and Protestant countries, whether the people are generally hostile to the Church or not, we are faced with the same essential problem. The Church is something standing away from the world, something unknown, something secret. It is a specialist affair for special people. It wears an official, professional air which is not "for the likes of us".

In "Catholic" countries the Church may be more familiar and its importance is more widely realized, but it is more readily disliked for its clericalism and its detachment from the most vexing problems of life. In "Protestant" countries, it is often respected and even looked up to for a solution of certain moral problems; but beyond this there is often a general indifference to it easily turning to active criticism when its teaching is resented. In either case, should it grow powerful and apparently rich, *e.g.* in Spain or in America, it sets up bitter hostility, even if it also obtains strong backing.

Catholics, too, while still practising their religion regularly or irregularly, can feel themselves to be separated, as though by a screen, from the clerical and official Church. They belong to the Church and they know that it is important in their lives, yet their worship remains external, not so much because they are indifferent to spiritual matters, but because the Church, as they see it, seems a self-contained, complex "thing" outside most of their lives, save for certain dated and defined purposes. They benefit rather than belong, while those who are more interested tend to attach themselves by external links of good works and devotions rather than from within, since there is no visible way within.

The problem has been widely recognized by alert Catholic minds, though as yet it does not greatly worry the majority of the clergy and laity in countries where the tragedy of the situation is not obvious, and the attempt to meet it has come either in the form of bringing the priest nearer to the people, whether paganized or still Catholic, or in the form of trying to establish more links of service to the priest from the people.

The priest is being brought nearer to the people to-day in many striking ways. Radio and television are two channels of publicity that must have done something to make the Church better understood. In less spectacular ways, ours has been an age when more and more small churches and chapels have brought the Mass to the people, and this work has been helped by motor travelling chapels. Even advertising and instruction by correspondence are being used with success.

But all these methods, necessary and immensely valuable as they may be, are limited in scope. They do not really break down the wall between Church and people. What they do is to draw the attention of the *individual* non-Catholic or restore the practice of religion of the *individual* Catholic. They make converts and they make better Catholics, but they neither bring the Church nearer the common life of the people nor do they prevent the drift or leakage from the Church among those affected by a secularist environment.

It is difficult to say that there are any new methods available for bringing the people nearer to the priests, except in so far as rather more opportunity is slowly being given to the Catholic laity itself to serve the Church with its brains, its technical competence, its secular training and so on. But apart from writers, journalists, teachers and lay catechists, there is at present little scope for initiative, and all such work tends to have a "clericalized" character. Those who work as Catholics in these fields acquire something of the "separate" or "apart" character which the Church generally has in public estimation, both Catholic and non-Catholic.

It seems evident that the clue to the problem of surmounting the wall separating Church from people must lie elsewhere. It must lie somehow in realizing that the lay Catholic, called to live his Christianity in the world, possesses *his own* responsible spiritual function *within* the Church. It is not a question only of bringing the priest nearer to individual people, or of bringing individual people nearer to the priest: it is a question of a living partnership, a living co-operation, a fellowship between the clergy and the laity, each with its special call and vocation within the Mystical Body of Christ. The priest has his sacred and unique rôle in the Mystical Body. This is universally understood. But the layman is no less fully responsible, fully active, fully following Christ's call to sanctification, because he belongs to the world. In finding his Christianity in the world, rather than trying to belong to two worlds, a "Church" world where he has no active rôle and a "worldly" world where he has no religion, must he witness to Christ in his life. It is this conception that needs active encouragement, rather than the conception of a clerical spirituality, if the separation between Church and people is to be overcome. For it is the layman, not the priest, who belongs to the people who to-day in their masses are hostile to the Church or indifferent to it, looking upon it as a remote, special and official "thing".

This truth has, of course, been widely recognized. It is at the heart of the modern liturgical movement, initiated by St

Pius X, a movement even now so often misunderstood as being little more than a matter of better singing and better rubrics. It is at the heart of the theological and intellectual renaissance which has owed so much to Pope Leo XIII, as it is also at the heart of the great social movement which we also owe to the same Pontiff and to his successors. Above all, perhaps, it finds its expression in Catholic Action. But even so it is as yet far from being widely understood.

Those who know anything of the work and methods of the Jeunesse Ouvrière Catholique (JOC and YCW), and movements akin to it, realize that in them we have lay Catholics, living responsible lay Catholic lives fully in the world. In the YCW, Catholic youth carries Christian (not pious or devout) principles of life and work into the most socially important of contemporary fields, the factory and the workshop. Youth is not there in a preaching or teaching capacity, but *in its natural and normal worker capacity*, by which in any case it must live its life, spiritual and temporal. In the beginning of such Catholic Action movements, it is necessary for members to have a special training in the spiritual and social witness of the Church so that they can carry by example, conversation, leadership in their work and their responsibilities the values and experience of fully lived Christianity. This is because Catholic education and training generally is still conceived in the old terms of religion being essentially a private affair with particular relevance to not missing Mass on Sundays and paying particular attention to the sixth and ninth commandments on weekdays, if you want to save your soul. Not the world, but personal life and the physical church are, in this view, the essential field of the Christian life. But it is permissible to hope and believe that with the wider realization of all that is implied in the liturgical, intellectual and social movements within the Church, the present specialization of Catholic Action and the extra training which it needs, perhaps even with a form of community life at any rate for the leaders, will become less necessary. For at bottom Catholic life and Catholic action are one and the same thing, as I shall hope to show in the following pages.

Meanwhile, no one can doubt how much has been owed and is being owed to the various types of specially organized lay apostolic endeavour in our times. This movement, apart from its hammering at the wall separating Church from people, has a double advantage. It does much to raise the level of genuine spiritual life among Catholics themselves, and this in a manner suited to the lay status, and it encourages more and more Catholics to imitate the example of how to live the Christian life in an effective apostolic way in the midst of a pagan and indifferent world. Up to a point the layman has begun to replace the priest without becoming semi-clericalized. Not only is the priest left more free to fulfil the sacramental and pastoral rôle which is his already and of which there is ever greater need, but a thousand witnesses to Christ have sprung up to replace a single one.

Yet a great deal of what is called "Catholic Action" is not so much a direct, responsible, lay Catholic witness from within the world, as a mode of helping the bishop and priest in their clerical administrative rôles. Most Catholic societies have for their object the furtherance of the Church's rule, the protection of the Catholic interests of Catholic members of different professions, helping in parish and diocesan work, and so on. Such bodies are necessary and valuable, but they do not in themselves bridge Church and world, Church and people. As leaders and active workers in such societies, Catholics share the strangeness of the Church in the eyes of the world, and, as things are, they tend to create the class of what I would call the "clericalist layman". The "clericalist layman" believes that only the priest can do real Christian work, and he wants to help him. Hence he is inclined to conceive of the work of the lay apostolate as being a kind of pale reflection of the priestly apostolate, and this view is often shared by priests. The fallacy is most easily detected in Catholic school or parish, where the "pious" child, the "sacristy" child, is picked out as the promising Catholic child, where the members of pious sodalities, always at the priests' beck and call, are the model parishioners. The person who will not move a finger without consulting the priest is taken as a model of Catholic reliability and obedience. At a higher stage it is the Catholic leader who is in and out of Catholic chancelleries and whose mind is dominated by ecclesiastical lore, correct rubrics, episcopal instruction, who tends to have responsibility and influence. In fact, there can come into existence something like a race apart of semi-clericalized laity whose virtues and talents, great as they may be, are usually the ones least suited to impress the outside world. In the matter of piety, what St Ignatius called "discernment of spirit" is more difficult. Later chapters will, I trust, show that I am very far from decrying piety and devotion, but the taste for retreats, extra devotions, presbyteries and convents, is not *in itself* and *by itself* a test of the quality of spiritual vitality and toughness which makes the most effective witness to truth in the contemporary world. And these do often seem to mark the clericals, male and female, I have in mind.

Strangely enough, all this derives, not from a sense of the real and vital spiritual *unity* between priest and layman, but from a false sense of separateness between them. The lay clerical race, feeling itself *separate* from an idea of fuller Catholicity realized only in the priesthood, wants to imitate it and wants somehow to get as close to it as possible. Since it cannot possibly achieve this, it seems to be condemned to live in a grey limbo of its own where both priestly apostolic effectiveness and lay apostolic effectiveness are impossible.

It may be that I have exaggerated the danger of this lay clericalism, but if I have done so it is because its existence is in a way symbolic of the essential point I should like to make in these chapters. Weighing the enormous responsibility that must, as I see it, fall to the laity if the wall that to-day separates Church from the masses is to be broken down, it seems to be necessary to show how the lay Christian apostolic vocation differs sharply from the priestly one. In a way the realization of this is something new in the Church, for the conditions of Christianity in the world of to-day are also something new. We live in the era of post-Christianity.

In the early Church, Christians formed groups or communities within a pagan society, and Christianity spread by a quality of enthusiastic preaching, example and suffering which was catching. In its freshness, beauty and revolutionary quality, it simply caught on. There was, as it were, a natural disposition within which the Holy Spirit could operate spectacularly. The danger was division and heresy. Gradually and necessarily, the Church consolidated itself, achieving the essential ecclesiastical shape we know to-day, for self-defence, for the assurance of inner unity and order, and for the conversion of the less sophisticated peoples who filled the void left by the decay of the Roman Empire.

With the conversion of these militant people, Christendom was unified by a strongly developed hierarchical principle which controlled faith, devotion and learning, while the temporal order, essentially subject to the Church, though often seeking to challenge its claims, was in the hands of autonomous Christian princes. In these conditions of universal rule of the civilized world and the flourishing of an essentially clerical culture, the people's ideas were closely assimilated to the clerical rule with the choice, so to speak, of heaven or hell as the sanction for personal conduct.

Then came the long period of humanism, corrupting much of the ecclesiastical world and setting both clergy and laity along new paths of discovery and culture, with the consequences of the religious divisions of Christendom and ultimately the emergence of new ideologies such as Nationalism, Liberalism, Socialism and Communism.

During this period the Church was under challenge throughout, and its energies were directed to saving the faith of the exposed Catholics and recovering that of those who had broken away. Only in the later stages of this development did it become clear that the mass of the people were settling down passively to a society and life that was in effect Godless and completely secularized. Their religious and moral ideals had been diverted to the making of better and juster human societies according to the conflicting prescriptions of the new secularist moral and social leaders. In recent years, this situation has tended to stabilize itself into the conflict between Communism and the "free" world. Within it, the Catholic Church has also tended to settle down to the double task of leading the spiritual fight against Communism and winning back the secularized masses of the "free" world to Christ.

These are the challenges of the era of post-Christianity in the areas of the world that had once been Christian or intimately affected by Christian civilization. Of their nature, they present quite a new problem of the laity. They do so, in the first place, because the laity is called upon to live its life, not merely in an environment unprecedented because of its religious indifference, but in daily intimate relationship of work and partnership with men and women often wholly alien to its spiritual and often moral values. At the same time, these people are by no means devoid of much genuine idealism and goodness. And in the second place, the laity is directly called by its Christian faith to go out and teach, in the name of the Father, Son and Holy Ghost, all with whom it comes into contact.

In such conditions it cannot be enough, as it was so often in the past, for a layman, in part clericalized by a special choice or taste of his, to be a kind of agent of the hierarchically organized and priestly ecclesiastical institution which the world knows of as a thing apart. It is true that the clergy, thus aided by selected layfolk, can bring many to the truth, as yearly conversion statistics prove. But measured by the size of the task to be accomplished, the number of such conversions is infinitesimal, and probably no greater than the number of those who drift away from the Church because of their secularized environment. Moreover, even were the number much larger, this method would still leave the world as the world sharply divided from the Church as the Church.

What is needed, rather, is an apostolic laity gradually coming to influence and change the texture of values of the world and thus preparing it, however remotely, for that change of mind and heart which will dispose it, socially as well as individually, to grace. One may also note here the evident fact that if the materialist and totalitarian ideology of Communism is to be finally overcome, this can only be done by a Christian penetration of this kind, since, as things are, the "free" world has, as a world, lost the sense of conviction of a spiritual order within which alone freedom can flourish sufficiently and be translated into firm institutions and relations powerful enough to challenge the attraction and logical development of Communism.

In order to work effectively towards such an end, the laity must come to feel that it possesses within itself a *certain Christian autonomy and status* that is different from that of the clergy, while springing equally directly from the Church which is the Mystical Body of Christ, all of whose members are equally centred in Almighty God and all inspired by the same Spirit.

This, of course, is always the case, but the accidents of history have until our own day tended to obscure the fact, or at least the inferences to be drawn from it.

If there is an age of the Church which corresponds most nearly to our own it is that of the early Church in which the New Testament emphasizes so clearly both the ecclesiastically authoritative and God-founded function of the chosen Apostles, together with their successors, and *the living community of the faithful* which corresponds to and completes the Body of Christ. It is St Paul who teaches: "We too, all of us, have been baptized into a single body by the power of a single Spirit, Jews and

Greeks, slaves and freemen alike; we have all been given drink at a single source, the one Spirit." [1]

The importance attached to this sense of unity within difference of function, and of community or fellowship, is attested again and again in such Scriptural phrases as "brotherhood", "same charity", "united in mind and judgment", "co-partners in Jesus", and in the common life and sharing of those times.

Such was the Christian mind and life in the face of the pagan world. For historical reasons, briefly suggested above, the Church was obliged to stress the vital importance of the authority and separateness of those whom Christ chose and ordained: the Apostles with Peter as their head and their successors. Because of this, the importance of community and fellowship in Christ tended to be understressed so that the Church has appeared through the ages more as a hierarchy and objective institution in touch with the temporal world and individual souls than as a community of Christ's members. But now that the Church is once again face to face with a world whose spiritual characteristic is the post-Christian secularization, we have seen a great return to the sense and theology of community in the liturgical movement and the realization of the meaning of the Mystical Body. But this change has not as yet widely applied its theological basis to the field of apostolic action and life, and its implications have hardly penetrated to the great majority of the faithful, including even many engaged in some form of Catholic Action.

In the following chapters I hope to suggest at least, and in an informal way, some of those implications.

[1] I Cor. 12. 13.

II

THE LAY STATUS

1. THE LAY PRIEST

HAVING inveighed so sharply against what I have called the "clericalist layman", it may seem somewhat paradoxical if I now embark on matters which establish the point that the clergy and the laity are, in fact, far more closely linked within the Church than is usually realized. But there is no paradox. The "clericalist layman", as I have said, is someone who feels himself to be different from a superior species whose conditions of life are perhaps too hard for him to bear ; someone who has entered upon commitments incompatible with the priesthood, and wishes to make the best of both worlds for himself by trying to be like the priest he cannot be and to live in as close an association with him as possible. On the other hand, there are far more of the laity who neither feel any sense of oneness with the priest, nor want to feel any. They are content to be citizens of the world, while needing the occasional services of the priest to save their souls or sign a form. For that matter, they feel for their fellow Catholics little more than perhaps a sense of shared loyalty to a common minority cause and the physical contiguity which worshipping in the same building involves.

Both types are in the wrong. The Catholic layman is most intimately bound with the priest, and this in sense far deeper than the universal Catholic realization that we are all Catholics together whose final destiny will be determined by our conduct rather than by any ecclesiastical status here below. And it is from this sense of deep unity that comes the realization of the vital apostolic difference of the Christian priestly and the Christian lay life.

Speaking to all Christians, whether clerical or lay, within only a few years of Our Lord's death, St Peter wrote: "You must be a holy priesthood, to offer up that spiritual sacrifice which God accepts through Jesus Christ"—and again, "You are a chosen race, a royal priesthood, a consecrated nation, a people God means to have for himself; it is yours to proclaim the exploits of the God who has called you out of darkness into his marvellous light."[1] In other words, *all* Christians are priests, kings and teachers or prophets.

In one obviously very important respect the distinction we usually make between the clergy (priests, bishops, authoritative teachers) and the people immediately disappears. Let us try to see what this means and how it can be.

Our community, our fellowship, with Christ who is Priest, King and Teacher or Prophet gives us our common status. But words like community and fellowship are far too weak to describe the relation of all Christians to Christ. "Oneness with", "incorporation with", are nearer the mark, for all members of Christ's Church are members or cells of the Mystical Body of which Christ is the Head. We are all one in Christ whose Incarnation as Man living in Palestine for some thirty years is mystically prolonged for all time in the Church He founded so that its members, raised to the dignity of sharing with Christ in this life, should be enabled with Christ's help to overcome the weakness of human nature and enjoy the full realization and vision of God in eternity. And what is true for us as mortal individuals is true for human history as a whole since Christ will come again in glory, thus completing the great Divine drama of the creation of man.

What does the word "priest" mean? It has in fact been used for different rôles, but its fundamental Christian meaning is one which relates itself to "sacrifice", that is, "making sacred". A sacrifice in ordinary language is a "giving up". We give up something we cherish for another whom we love or towards whom we feel an obligation. In the religious sense, the sacrifice we may make in life for another becomes a sacrifice made to God because, as creatures, we recognize an obligation to God, a duty to worship and serve and love and give thanks to God. In particular, that need to sacrifice is recognized when we feel the need to "make up" to God for our failure to serve Him properly, *i.e.* for our sins. To offer up such sacrifice, whether of some symbolic gift, or of ourselves, is a priestly act. This is true even of the natural order. But the whole idea of sacrifice and priesthood was given a new and infinitely superior significance when God Himself became Man and offered Himself up to the

[1] I Peter 2. 5, 9.

Eternal Father for the sins of the whole world. Any sacrifice to God which a mere man can make is necessarily a highly imperfect sacrifice since the best which man can offer can bear no comparison with all-Reality and all-Perfection of the Godhead. But when God Himself became Man and offered up Himself, the sacrifice was perfect and supreme. God's infinite love had found a means of reconciling mankind to God, of making atonement, which literally means at-one-ment, making one again. In this supreme sacrifice, Christ who is God was and remains the priest, the fullness of priesthood, the High Priest. "He would be a High Priest who could feel for us and be our true representative before God, to make atonement for the sins of the people."[1] Christ, having thus effected the reconciliation of fallen man with the Godhead, established on earth the visible community or Church which was Himself distributing by certain ordained means the fruits of His sacrifice which was to be mystically repeated in the Church for all time in the Sacrifice of the Mass. But the Divine touch gave a new value and meaning to all who were to be, and are, incorporated in His Body, the Church, by baptism.

Every Christian has thus been made priest with Christ in every spiritual sacrifice which he makes right up to his own supreme self-sacrifice, should he be called upon to make it, the sacrifice of his life in witness of Christ in martyrdom. "True sacrifice is to be found in every deed done with a view to union with God in a holy communion, that is, every act that is referred to the end that can make us truly blessed", wrote St Augustine. In fact, the whole of our spiritual lives as Catholics are in an absolutely true sense *priestly* lives.

Furthermore, Christ at the Last Supper said "Do this in commemoration of me" and in doing so gave power to His Apostles, and to all to whom the Apostles would hand on the power, to change the bread and wine into the Body and Blood of Christ in the Sacrifice of the Mass. The power to act in the name of Christ in offering the Sacrifice of the Mass is reserved to the *ordained* priest, the priest ordained at the hands of the bishop, as the bishop was consecrated by another bishop until we reach back to the Apostles whose consecration and ordination were at the hands of Christ. But though at Mass it is only the *ordained* priest who possesses the sacred power to represent Christ, the High Priest, in renewing the Sacrifice of Calvary,

[1] Hebrews 2. 17.

the faithful represent the whole Church by their prayers and their offerings, chiefly of course of themselves, and in doing so apply the fruits of the sacrifice to the whole community of the Church which includes priests and the faithful. "My sacrifice and yours", says the priest turning to the people, and the ritual throughout demands the co-prayers of the faithful and their assent.

The prayers and ritual make it clear that the Mass is in no way a private prayer, whether for celebrant or faithful. It is the prayer and act of the Church, wherein, as in High Mass, different kinds of priestly or sacrificial rôles are played: celebrant, deacon, subdeacon, acolytes, choir and faithful. In modern times, the lesser rôles are usually taken by ordinary layfolk, and in religious communities monks or clerks without even minor orders can take the high rôle of subdeacon. In Jesuit schools this is (or was) commonly done. Here, therefore, we have another sense, and a very important one, in which the laity are priests. Apart from their *spiritual* priesthood in making spiritual sacrifices in their own spiritual lives as members of Christ's Body, they have a *sacramental*, though lesser, priestly rôle in the central act of Christian worship, the Sacrifice of the Mass.

At first sight, all this may be rather confusing. Does it only mean that the layman is a kind of metaphorical priest? Or, on the other hand, does it mean that less importance should be attached to the priesthood of the ordained priest? It means neither. Such questions can only arise from the too common misunderstanding of the nature of the Church.

The one same Church of Christ may be viewed in two lights. We can think of it as an order or institution founded by Christ with powers delegated by Christ to different persons in it according to different needs. And we can also think of it as the fellowship of all its members in Christ. If one likes, one can think of it as from above downwards or from below upwards. The ordained priest, in his priestly powers and functions, has a special place in the spiritual order or hierarchy of the Church, though as an individual Christian he belongs, as we all do, to the fellowship in Christ. The layman as priest has no place in that hierarchy and he possesses no special priestly powers. But as a member of the Christian community he is in a priestly, sacrificing communion with Christ and all the members of the Church from the Pope downwards.

We know that the handing over to the priest in sacramental ordination of the power to say Mass and consecrate also confers other powers, not least that of giving absolution in confession and administering the last sacraments. In fact, the priesthood of the laity makes no *visible* difference to the picture of the Church as we all know it. But the realization of the priesthood of the laity by the laity could make a great difference to their own feelings about themselves as members of the Church.

It would make them understand the enormous spiritual dignity of being a Catholic at all and the closeness of their union with Christ the High Priest. Instead of the all too common idea of being "also rans" in Christianity, separate somehow from the " officials", and consequently having minor religious responsibilities, they would understand that we are all together, co-operators, not in a merely utilitarian sense when circumstances demand it, but in the very essence and meaning of the Christian faith. And most of all it would make clear that just as the ordained priesthood, with all that goes with it, involves one way of Christian life, one type of apostolate, one form of spiritual living, so the priesthood of the laity involves for all *its* type of apostolate and *its* form of spiritual living, not apart from the world, but in the world in a way neither normally open to the ordained priest nor suited to his special vocation. And in case any reader should still think that all this is a kind of fancy doctrine dug out by speculative theologians, let me end this section by quoting the confirming words of Pope Pius XII in the encyclical *Mediator Dei*: "By reason of their baptism Christians are in the Mystical Body and become by a common title members of Christ the Priest: by the 'character' that is graven upon their souls they are appointed to the worship of God, and, therefore, according to their condition, they share in the priesthood of Christ Himself."[1]

2. THE LAY PROPHET

Surprising as the universal Christian priesthood or the priesthood of the laity may seem to some, it may not come as quite so much of a shock as another attribute of the laity, perhaps because priesthood is not a very easy thing to understand, save in terms of the separate powers of the ordained priest.

[1] Paragraph 92.

But if there is one thing that we normally attribute to the laity, it is the part of "being taught", "being instructed", looking to Pope, bishops and priests for doctrine and knowledge about God. The layman is ignorant of these things, and it is for the clergy in authority, with a specialized knowledge of its own, to tell him what he ought to know and ought to think. And all this, of course, is absolutely true. The Pope and bishops are our teachers, the "teaching Church". This great responsibility is a direct commission from Christ to Peter and the Apostles and to their successors. It is theirs to guard and draw out the original "deposit of faith". It is their responsibility, too, to train and instruct the clergy to pass on that faith to their people and to exhort them to live it as it should be lived. But we grow a queer habit of supposing that because something is absolutely true, there is nothing more to be said. We think of things in terms of "either, or". *Either* the clergy teaches, *or* the faithful teach; but the faithful obviously do not teach in the usual sense of the word; therefore the clergy alone teaches. The true position is more much complex and subtle. It is truer to say that the hierarchy with the aid of the clergy teach in one way *and* the faithful teach in another.

On reflection it will be seen that this truth is even easier to understand than the priesthood of the laity. For whereas our priesthood springs from the priesthood of Christ, our teaching not only springs from the prophetic or inspirational power of Christ in whom we are all incorporated, but it is also derived from our relation with the Holy Spirit whom Our Lord promised and sent to the Church at Pentecost, as He sends Him to each of us individually in the sacraments, especially of Baptism and Confirmation. Christ is the "light who enlightens every soul born into the world"[1] and the Epistles testify again and again to the light, grace, inspirations and gifts which the Holy Spirit gives to every Christian soul. It is because of this that every Christian lives a *witness* to the truth, the faith, derived from God within him, Christ of whom he is a member, and the Spirit who inspires him. We realize the fact once it is pointed out, but we have grown so accustomed to thinking only of the authoritative teaching rôle of the hierarchical Church that we even tend to forget that unless there was a supernatural capacity within each one of us to be witnesses of the Christ within us, the Church's teaching would be meaning-

[1] John 1. 9.

less, as indeed it is to those who have not been born again in the Spirit.

Once again we have to distinguish between the Church in its aspect of a hierarchical teaching institution, guaranteeing the faith and preserving all from error, and the Church in its aspect of a community in the living Christ, of members in whom God dwells by grace and whom the Holy Spirit ever teaches and inspires. What this latter aspect meant in the early Church is described by St Paul in the first epistle to the Corinthians.

The revelation of the Spirit is imparted to each, to make the best advantage of it. One learns to speak with wisdom, by the power of the Spirit, another to speak with knowledge, with the same Spirit for his rule; one, through the same Spirit, is given faith; another, through the same Spirit, powers of healing; one can perform miracles, one can prophesy, another can test the spirit of the prophets; one can speak in different tongues, another can interpret the tongues; but all this is the work of one and the same Spirit, who distributes his gifts as he will to each severally.[1]

These special graces or gifts, charismata, as they are called, were needed by the infant Church, and so the Holy Spirit gave them at that time. But the inspirations and gifts continue for each one of us in an inner, rather than an external, way, even though throughout the history of the Church saints and exceptional souls have manifested in miracles and revelations similar special powers and inspirations. And these, of course, have been distributed quite irrespective of the clerical or lay status of the individuals so privileged. And, just as the hierarchical teaching Church preserves and guarantees faith, so it judges whether miracles and revelations are truly so—whether they come from God and in what degree of directness and with what authority so far as the rest of us are concerned.

Apart from such revelations manifested to the world, we have also the immense record of mystical contemplation in which countless souls have been given a direct intimacy with God, an experience of Him, which, though falling far short of the Beatific Vision in heaven and remaining within the order of faith, goes far beyond the conceptual and opaque knowledge of God which the rest of us can only hope to have.

[1] I Cor. 12. 7–11.

In all this, no doubt, we are dealing with exceptional cases, but there is nothing whatever exceptional in the *witness* we are all of us obliged to give of the truth that is *in us*.

In being Christians, we willy-nilly teach Christianity, whether we teach it well or teach it badly. There is little that we can say and less perhaps that we can do which is not a Christian sermon to those among whom we live and work, or a betrayal of the trust which the Holy Spirit has put into us.

The sermon may be preached to non-Catholics or it may form part of that constant intercommunion between those who together are members of Christ and in duty bound to support one another in love and mutual example.

Nor can this be understood in merely a general sense. It has to be understood in terms of our separate calls and vocations. The world is necessarily dependent on men and women filling different functions because God created nature "virgin", a raw material, as it were, of animal, vegetable and mineral for man to use and fulfil. Only so can the potentialities of the divine creative power be brought out. And man himself is a social creature whose natural development in mind and body is impossible save through receiving from and giving back to nature and to his fellow men. Our Lord Himself in His years of manual work, in His miracles and cures, and in His parables exhorting His followers to trust the divine creation and to use their talents, gave us the example. A combination of factors, no doubt, decides what job we take, what kind of work in life we shall do, but one of those factors should always be our own special potentiality which we discover in heredity, taste, ability, appetite and so on. In this there is always a natural grace ready to be supernaturalized into the true "grace of state" which enables us not only to do the job we are doing as well as our abilities will allow, but to act within them with the *authority* to be witnesses to God's will and plan, and thus, in our own way, however humble, to be prophets and teachers. This seems specially true of the basic vocations of parent, child, husband and wife, and of vocations which are directly auxiliary to those, for example, in the field of education and training, and of vocations that minister to essential human needs, for example, doctors and those who grow or draw from the earth our primary needs of food, shelter, clothes, or those who minister to our minds and senses in literature, art, music. But it is also true of all.

Apart from all this teaching and witnessing to God's truth and plan, to Christ's revelation and to the work of the Holy Spirit—the Godhead to which we are so intimately bound— we have a teaching potentiality which links itself with the teaching authority of the Church that resides in the Pope and bishops. For the preaching and the teaching of the Faith are delegated, not only directly to the clergy, but indirectly to many of the laity. Catholic parents, for example, are teachers of their children in early youth both in virtue of a parenthood which has its own "grace of state", and in virtue of an undefined commission of the Church which looks to parents to bring up their children in the Faith. Equally, the Church looks to Catholic teachers to play a vital part in religious instruction where this is needed. And whether directly in the field of Catholic action proper or indirectly (by approval and consent) in the nowadays immensely wide field of Catholic activity in the worlds of politics, social questions, literature, art, more and more Catholics are being called in to be teachers who depend upon and extend in some way the authority and magisterium of the Church.

In saying all this, we are not, as readers will perceive for themselves, saying anything new. But most of us are content to accept the facts as just facts which we take for granted. What we fail to appreciate is how these facts link up in the most intimate manner possible with the Church and therefore with Christ.

We are not just lone individuals thrown into the world and having to maintain exterior and accidental links with a Church "over there" when it is a question of specifically spiritual and moral matters; we spring directly from the centre which is Christ and we are linked together in the Body which is Christ. We receive together and individually the inspiration of the Spirit of God.

Hence, just as our incorporation with Christ makes us all *priests*, so it makes us all *teachers* with and of Christ so that all we say and do in our lives possesses a virtue and grace of its own, springing immediately from our membership of the Church. Nor is this virtue and grace any less of a virtue and grace than the teaching *authority* of the Church, even though it is to be sharply distinguished from it. To that teaching authority we look for the Faith and order which Christ specially entrusted to it and for the ruling which will tell us when *we* are teaching and witnessing rightly. It is indeed obvious that our minds and talents, especially under the influence of our fallen wills and appetites, are only too capable of abusing and neglecting the inspiration and grace that are offered to us.

3. THE LAY KING

Then there is a third main way in which the incorporation of the faithful in Christ endows them with a dignity and function that is too easily overlooked, even though we have become devotionally so familiar with the title of Christ from which this position springs. The institution of the feast of Christ the King reminds us all of Christ's authority—authority over the Church; authority over every soul created by God; authority over the world.

That kingly authority of Christ is also exercised in His Mystical Body of which we are all members, and consequently we all in some sense share Christ's kingly authority. "Thou hast made us a royal race of priests, to serve God; we shall reign as kings over the earth." [1]

Christ's royal authority is most obviously and directly manifested in the ecclesiastical authority and government of the Church, exercised by the Pope and the bishops, by Our Lord's own direct commission and to which we are all subject. But this which we all recognize by no means limits the manifestation of Christ's authority in the world. Christ is not only King of the Church; He is also King of the world. In fact, as He Himself laid down, the exercise of Divine authority in this world is a divided one: "Render to Caesar the things that are Caesar's and to God the things that are God's." This division creates a problem. Though Christ is King of the world, He has not delegated His royal power to secular rulers in the direct way He has delegated it to spiritual rulers, even though at times in the history of Christendom temporal rule under a consecrated emperor seemed to balance spiritual rule under a consecrated pope.

By their nature, temporal concerns admit of an indefinite variety of social and personal behaviour, whereas spiritual and moral concerns are fixed. There is only one spiritual order and there is only one moral code. This order and this code affects the Church through and through since the Church exists to

[1] Apocalypse 5. 10.

witness to it and defend it. And in so far as it is applicable to temporal affairs, it must still be in the hands of the Church which to this day claims an *indirect* power over temporal governments and affairs. This means that the Church claims to tell the whole world what is spiritual and moral truth and, in so far as it is capable of doing so, to enforce it through secular rulers. But even if the Church were in a position actively to enforce its spiritual and moral authority over and through temporal governments, these governments would still be responsible for the *temporal* ways and means, in politics, sociology, economics and administration generally, of ensuring the best good in secular matters of the people entrusted to them. In point of fact, the Church's temporal indirect power has become no more than a claim since the secular world no longer recognizes it. Being, like all Christianity, essentially a power *in conscience*, and not a tyranny or armed power, the denial by free men of the Church's claim makes it impotent. But the moral law is a law of reason, to be read in every straight-thinking human conscience, whether that conscience knows of Christ's revelation or not. Consequently, the duty of man to obey the fundamental moral dictates of conscience is universal, and it is with God's authority that temporal governments and peoples enforce the moral law on which temporal authority and order themselves depend.

The whole world is God's Kingdom in this sense and all men, according to their responsibilities, are God's delegates in exercising that Divine authority. More deeply still, all human self-control and control of the nature created by God for man is a delegation of the control which the Creator wields over His own creation.

But once a man has become a Christian, that is, once he has been incorporated in Christ, all this Divine Kingship and authority are understood in a new light and exercised in a new and far more significant way.

It is now seen to spring from Christ the King—Christ who was Man among men, Christ who prolonged Himself in the order of space and time in the Church which is His Mystical Body, Christ with whom all Christians together and each Christian singly are intimately bound in supernatural grace. The authority which each of us wields within the natural order that God created is raised to the level of a Christian responsibility. For Christ in reconciling man to God and revealing the full truth about our eternal destiny and the place of the world in the divine plan has called us to be His agents, His delegates, in the work of achieving His Kingdom—the Kingdom into which He will come again at the last day in glory. For, though God is king of all that *is*, this fallen world, so much in the hands of man's freedom to choose evil instead of good, cannot be an ordered Kingdom until at the last day the evil is separated away from the good and God's justice and authority have been finally and publicly vindicated.

One can understand, therefore, the supernatural significance of everything that members of Christ's Mystical Body accomplish even in the temporal or secular order. However much their actions and responsibilities may seem to be removed from spiritual matters, they are still building *with Christ* what will be God's completed work. The authority they wield, whether it be conspicuous in the eyes of the world or so humble as to be no more than control of self and of the nature they use, is always a spiritual authority.

We can now better understand how it was that in the ages of faith monarchs were consecrated by the Church, not as is sometimes suggested to a kind of sacerdotal status, but as men solemnly set apart for their office and vowed to exercise it justly and with the consent of their fellow members in Christ over whom they must rule. Equally, the Church, realizing the Christian importance of temporal concerns, took dominion through some of its prelates over civil responsibilities. While, through the weakness of human nature, this led to abuse, the principle itself when rightly exercised in exceptional circumstances was just. The temporal sovereignty of the Vicar of Christ, maintained to this very day, is an example of a special need to safeguard a minimum temporal independence for the free exercise of a spiritual authority specially commissioned by Christ for the maintenance of God's revealed truth which covers temporal as well as spiritual affairs.

There is no need here to recapitulate the well-known grounds of the direct spiritual authority of the Church exercised by Pope and bishops, but it is important to see how the faithful or laity generally share within the Church in the authority that derives from Christ's kingship.

We have already seen that all exercise of authority in temporal and natural matters is exercised in Christ and consequently within the fellowship of Christ which is the Church.

But this fellowship, this communitarianism, of all Christians in Christ is so close that the specific spiritual authority of the Church's magisterium in matters of faith and morals cannot be divorced from the faithful. The functions are different but the Church is one. Consequently all the faithful participate in the spiritual authority of Christ which the hierarchical Church exercises.

The basic ways, it would seem, are by agreement and by witness.

In the early Church and for many centuries, bishops were elected by the people, not of course in the sense that bishops derived their power and jurisdiction from the electing people as a president or deputy does in a democracy.

What the election did was to ensure the faithful's approval or consent to this or that person being invested with Christ-given powers by the method of choosing the most worthy. In the course of history this rôle of the people was assumed by their princes and rulers, who exercised it, not in the interests of the Church, but in their own. The history of Europe, and not least of England, offers many examples of the lamentable results of this abuse. With the Reformation the principle that the hierarchy is linked sacramentally to Christ, deriving its powers and authority solely from Him, was called in question. Consequently, the principle of election has been steadily narrowed, and finally has given way to that of Papal nomination for the final choice. But even so the consent of the faithful in the sense of a willing obedience to and co-operation with the bishop nominated by the Pope as most suited to the office is presupposed. A bishop ruling against the will of the faithful is inconceivable simply because there would be a rupture between the head and the members of the self-same "Church" —in the diocesan sense of the word.

In a similar way, the laity, in the persons of consultants or princely wielders of secular power, took part in oecumenical Church Councils until modern times. Princes and other laymen were not thought of as being part of the Council either for the establishing of dogma or the government of the Church, but as indispensable auxiliaries and representatives of the *consent* of the Church to the decisions in the sense that the living fellowship of all Christians in Our Lord was one with the hierarchical decisions. In our own day, we have an analogous authoritative rôle of the laity in the consent, indeed petition, of the faithful that the dogma of the Assumption be defined by the Pope. Here is a clear case where the aid of the Holy Spirit in each member of Christ, as in the Church as a whole, results in a decision of the highest authoritative character. It may be said, too, that any Christian, whether clerical or lay, is in a position actively to co-operate in all that goes towards establishing what is pronounced by hierarchical authority to be a matter of faith and morals or a matter of liturgical devotion. This may be done by prayer, study, writing, organizing, petitioning. And in the case of such important liturgical devotions as those of the feast of the Blessed Sacrament and the feast of the Sacred Heart, the movement came from women saints and was in due course approved and highly encouraged by Popes.

Lay participation in the kingly authority of Christ and the Church is also seen in lay *witness* to hierarchical authority. This is effected in a great variety of ways. Lay participation in Church Councils had for one of its express purposes the enforcing of decisions and spreading the news of them. This latter function has a special interest and appeals to me as a Catholic journalist, for it is a fact that but for Catholic papers there would be no effective way in the modern world of bringing to the universal Church the words of the Supreme Pontiff in his constant doctrinal and spiritual discourses. That is why Pope Pius XI insisted that Catholic newspapers were "the voice of the Pope". In a recent instance, the press was actually made the medium by which a vitally important disciplinary Constitution was made public. I refer to *Christus Dominus* which altered the law of the Eucharistic fast. Normally such a Constitution would be transmitted to the bishops, and from the bishops to the parish priests. But in this instance it was only made known by publication in the *Osservatore Romano* and the *Acta Apostolicae Sedis*, and from these to the Catholic papers of all the countries of the world.

We have already seen how Christ's kingly authority is shared by all who have responsibilities in civil life—and this in some degree includes everyone. But when we think specifically of the application of the Church's doctrine and moral teaching to temporal matters so closely related to the Church as, for example, Catholic education especially in non-Catholic countries, those engaged in the defence and realization of Catholic claims are in effect delegates of the Church's hierarchical authority. They are specifically so, if they are appointed by the bishops, and indirectly so if they are clearly working within their consent. Such work, moreover, is not purely passive, but often active in that the striking of the political and administrative bargains that are necessary may constitute, when the Church approves of them, a new situation in the Church's juridical system. Though such work is often shared between clergy and laity, with the major part falling to the clergy, the decisive action usually falls to the layman because he alone possesses the necessary political power.

Authority, which is so closely linked with teaching, is obviously exercised by parents, teachers, writers, those engaged in Catholic Action or Catholic activities in the world, artists, professional men, such as doctors and lawyers, and many others. Here again, we have to distinguish between those who have a specific commission from the hierarchical Church, the bishop or the priest acting as the bishop's delegate, and those who only work personally on their own authority within the Catholic fellowship. Those with a specific commission in formally constituted Catholic Action or, for example, as catechists, are very closely linked with the hierarchical authority, while the others derive their authority from the Catholicity that links them directly to Christ the King, though always in submission to the hierarchical Church through which He speaks for specific purposes. This may seem to be something of a legal distinction since the position in practice may seem rather confused. But it is important to make the distinction in order to avoid the danger of supposing that Catholic authority deriving from the fellowship of Catholics in Christ the King could in some way be thought of as a rival authority to that of the hierarchical Church. This would divide the Body of Christ. Instead its unity is expressed in its two aspects of a Christ-commissioned hierarchical and sacramental order and of a life of grace and responsibility shared by all in their incorporation with Christ.

4. THE LAY VOCATION

I have tried in this chapter briefly to explain, analyse and describe the three main principles that underlie the Christian status and dignity of the Catholic laity—and, of course, of the clergy as members of the Church, apart from their hierarchical or sacramental status. The three principles derive from the incorporation of all the faithful in the Body of Christ who is

Priest, Prophet or Teacher and King. In our lives of sacrifice, prayer and devotion we are priests with Christ the High Priest. In our active and secular lives as Catholics, we are teaching and authoritative witnesses with Christ the Prophet and Christ the King. This priestly, teaching and authoritative quality of the faithful is part and parcel of the Christian life in itself in fellowship with Christ. But we are also priests in a sacramental sense, especially in partaking in the Sacrifice of the Mass which the ordained priest offers in the place of Christ Himself. As teachers and kings, we are also closely bound to the teaching and authoritative rôle of the institutional hierarchical Church as consenting and witnessing to its divine commission and, in some cases, aiding it in its work and under its authority.

Once again, the reader may feel that, after all, I have said very little that is not obvious and elementary, once the main principles are stated. In the ordinary sense of the word, the laity are neither priests, nor teachers, nor rulers within the Church, and we have always known that we can pray, witness to Christ and rule at least ourselves and in our temporal rôles. But even the doctrine of the Mystical Body is still little known among the laity generally, and in so far as it is known, it sounds "mystical" in the sense of mysterious, hardly comprehensible.

To understand what it means we need to understand how we are all the time intimately linked with Christ *still* acting, *still* at work, through each generation of Christians who are one in Him. We need to understand that in every act of our lives that is in accordance with His will we *are* Christ ("I live now not I, but Christ lives in me"), Christ in prayer and sacrifice, Christ revealing and teaching His Father's Being and Will in all things, Christ exercising the Divine dominion and rule which shapes the pattern of the good life on earth and for the eternal realization of God's glory itself. We need, too, to understand how the Church is not only a visible institution standing, as it were, over against the world and divided between the commissioned, specialist, professional hierarchy and clergy and a passive, individualistic laity, but also the unity in everything of all its members in Christ, distinctions being ones of powers, vocations, functions according to God's plan.

There is no such thing as a passive or merely individual member of the Church. Every member shares all with all and possesses *his* active vocation within the unity of diversity, a vocation that is just as much a Christ-vocation in every sense of the word as is that of any other member of the Church, however exalted in function and rank.

One needs to see all this if one is to understand the vocation and rôle of the laity as a whole and one's own within it in particular, vocations and rôles absolutely distinct from those of the clergy in their clerical functions, yet one with them in the whole work of Christ prolonged in time in His Mystical Body which makes us all one. And from this distinction in unity must arise the understanding of the distinct spirituality and apostolicity of the laity within the one spirituality and apostolicity of the Church which is Christ.

To work this out in any depth and completeness would need far more space and far more knowledge and insight than the present lay writer possesses. All I can hope to do in later chapters is to sketch some lines of thought which may prove helpful.

III

LAY SPIRITUALITY

I. A SLOW DEVELOPMENT

Wᴇ have already noted that the history of the Church until modern times has created circumstances unfavourable to the development of a distinct lay spirituality and apostolate.

In fact, it is hardly too much to say that this development has had to wait for the evolution in history of a free and educated people trained to realize and accept social responsibilities within a stable society. One might be tempted to say a "democratic" society. But this would be misleading since we think of democracy in terms of political and parliamentary freedom, whereas its essence lies rather in cultural and economic social conditions which permit of the self-development of the human being in a sufficient personal independence from massive authorities, whether of State or Church—the latter in the historical sense of clerical power exercised over secular life. In democracies we believe that political and parliamentary freedom is a necessary condition of such satisfactory self-development. On paper we are right. But experience has certainly shown that parliamentary democracy in practice can very easily lead to a degree of abuse and corruption that cancels out the theoretic values which it claims to establish. Far more important than political self-government in what we call a democratic system is the establishment of cultural, social and economic freedoms which in theory are guaranteed by political liberty and yet in practice may be endangered by it. Thus while democracy has worked well in Anglo-Saxon countries, as well as in a few others, it seems to me that, all prejudices apart, greater cultural, social and economic freedom can for the time being be achieved under a benevolent authoritarianism in Spain than under democracy in Spain. The same may well be true in Eastern countries where democratic traditions have never been established. As for European countries like Italy and Germany, it can be suggested that the real freedoms there are insufficiently established to make it certain that they are best protected and developed under parliamentary democracy of the contemporary type. Some alternative political system might serve the real good of the people better.

However, this is by the way. The point is that we have needed the evolution towards essential human freedom and education to be able to work out and establish a clearly distinct form of lay spirituality springing from all that is implied in the doctrine of the Mystical Body of Christ which is the Church.

In the past, the Church has been faced by a world that was essentially uncultured, uneducated and unfree, or by a world which associated the development of culture, education and freedom with opposition to the Church. In fact it was the task of the Church in the West to re-form the barbarian society which came to replace the Roman civilization, and this task was necessarily done by its own clergy, secular and, chiefly, regular, which imposed its own learning and its own essentially clerical spirituality on the lay world. In so far as this provoked opposition from secular rulers, the secular world, still for the most part uncultured, either sided with the Church as its best defender or politically opposed its clerical ideal, save for a minimum observance of the essentials of religion to avoid the damnation which the Church proclaimed for unrepentant sinners.

Thus, in the Middle Ages, we have the picture of a clerically-formed secular society with magnificent achievements to its name in the way of theological and philosophical learning, in the way of artistic and architectural glories singing the praises of God, and in the way of a pattern of social and economic order which was translated into a decency and happiness of living more by the charity and love of the clerical system and the monasteries than by realizing its own social ideal in practice. Meanwhile, the laity itself remained uneducated, passive and subject to the extrinsic authority of Church and State. Its spiritual ideal was very much a reflection of the clerical and monastic ideal. The minority which wanted to attain to a high degree of spirituality imitated as far as it could the outlook of the monks; it rejected the world in favour of a separate spirituality and asceticism; and it tolerated as little as possible any worldly pleasure or satisfaction even in the licit and sacramental form of marriage. Another form of spiritual realization was in the defence of Christendom by arms, especially against the Saracens. The meeting of the two ideals was effected in the military semi-monastic orders of chivalry. But the majority, no doubt, were content to accept as much as they had a mind to do of the religious life which was embedded in the social institutions that governed so much of their existences. In such a clerical society their outward lives conformed to Catholicity, as it does in a country like Ireland to-day, but this could give little indication of the quality of their inner Catholic lives, apart from those who modelled themselves on the clerical and monastic spiritual ideal.

The beginnings of an authentic lay Catholicity came with the beginnings of the new learning, whose sources were secular rather than religious, thus producing an outstanding Catholic lay figure like St Thomas More, but the Reformation destroyed any chance of the development of this blending of Church and an autonomous Catholic society whose sources of culture and life were becoming non-clerical. The Church needed all the help it could get to defend the truth against heresy, and it launched its necessarily clerical counter-attack with the Jesuits and other new religious orders working for conversion within an increasingly troubled and divided secular society. Lay Catholics once again tended to be clericalized, though more by choice than environment, or they drifted into laxity and unbelief. It is interesting that at this time, as at times in the Middle Ages, a minority wanted to escape from the dilemma through the pursuit of mysticism which tends to establish a personal religious life transcending the secular order and removed to some extent from the normal discipline and devotion of the institutional Church.

But neither Catholicism nor Protestantism was destined to triumph in the course of the long conflict between them. Instead, the real victory went to secularism which increasingly developed temporal ideals or ideologies of its own. These have brought the world to the pass it is in to-day, rent by terrible wars, hot or cold, and totally unable to create a common belief upon which peace and order can rest. But, despite these ideological, national and economic conflicts of the era of the new wars of pseudo-religion, steady progress has been made in raising the standards of living, culture and personal freedom. Already, however, there are signs of retrogression because the masses find themselves more and more subjected to the impersonal rule of technology and the machine. This tendency is deliberately exploited by Communism, but it is becoming ever more marked even in democracies which profess to foster more humanist ideals.

Meanwhile, outside Communist-dominated countries, the secularist world retains a measure of moral idealism, of "good paganism" that is rooted in universal education, a standard of life higher than ever before and a greater measure of essential freedom in personal and social life. Though this culture is fundamentally divorced from any real supernatural religion and any effective belief in God and Revelation, despite a certain outward show of respect for Christian Churches, it is for the moment capable of being Christianized. How long that moment will last is very uncertain; it may not be so long as we like to imagine.

- Both Catholicism and Protestantism have sought to seize their opportunity of Christianizing the secularist free world. In this attempt, Protestantism possesses certain advantages. Precisely because of its flexibility, its nationalism, its adaptability to different conditions, its greater measure of laicism, and the quicker evolution of its thought to the ideological and scientific views of the day, it can more easily permeate the secularist world from within. We should not, for example, underrate its very real contribution to the social and democratic traditions of America, Britain and Scandinavia, which in this respect are in marked contrast with Latin Catholic countries where long clericalist battles have been fought and where Catholics tend to be opposed to the Government and the social administration. But the defects of the Protestant merits have proved on the whole to be fatal to success in re-Christianizing the secularist world. This divided and emasculated Christianity elicits too little response from a world that is content enough with its own secularist ideals until it hears of something radically different and carrying an authentic message from an altogether different order of reality and values. It is significant that Protestantism itself is turning away from Liberalism and Modernism and reverting to the stronger meat of the Gospels and sacramental system, and in so far as it does this, its appeal is more effective. But the more it does this, the more it looks like Catholicism, leaving the world to choose between one, universal, unchanging and unchanged Christian message and a divided, changing and apparently imitative one.

The field is therefore open to the Catholic Church, which has indeed over the last fifty years drawn from her treasury immense spiritual riches, strength and fervour so that she stands to-day in a position of great authority and prestige over against the post-Christian world. Lately, too, the increasing danger of materialistic Communism has caused millions to see in her a potent and necessary ally in re-establishing in the world a faith which can counter the Communist faith.

Nevertheless, the Catholic Church too has its difficulties in seizing full advantage of the present opportunities, which may not last indefinitely. How great these difficulties are may be measured both by the steady drift of its own members away from the Church—the leakage, as it is called; and by the relatively very small number of converts made, with most of these probably recruited from other Christian Communions rather than from the post-Christian world.

The realization of the size of the problem has been the cause of the great call in our times to the laity to help the clergy in the work of the apostolate, and this, we may be sure, is an innovation destined to increase steadily. As I have said, the laity to-day, who for the most part enjoy within the secular world an unprecedented degree of education, social status and personal independence or freedom, have the chance, as never before, of being active and autonomous auxiliaries in this apostolate in the way best suited to the Christian dignity and opportunity of the lay status within the fellowship of the Mystical Body. By fulfilling their rôle, *as laymen* rather than as Roman-collarless clericals, they could do much to solve the problem of converting the wall that separates the world from the clerical Church, as it too often appears to be, into a bridge between Christ and temporal society.

How this great opportunity can best be seized is a problem that still demands much study from both the clergy and the laity, for it is certain that it is the clergy which will have to educate and train the laity to its special apostolic rôle and to the spiritual formation that must underlie it. I have described in a previous book[1] what seem to me from my own experience as a Catholic to be the shortcomings of the formation which the laity usually receive in our schools and from our parishes. These shortcomings may perhaps be summed up by saying that the laity are taught a "simple" and rather *external* religion of moral observance and loyalty to the Church as an institution rather

[1] *Living Christianity* (Burns & Oates).

than an *inner* religion based on the spiritual meaning of the
liturgy and the sense of Catholic fellowship in Christ. Religion
as thus commonly taught corresponds to the prevailing idea of
division between clergy and laity, whereas an inner religion,
which, I have argued, is more spiritual and may prove far more
efficacious, corresponds to the idea of Christian unity between
clergy and laity expressing itself in practice in two different
types of vocation and apostolate.

2. RE-ORDERING NATURE

Evidently the first expression of this lay vocation and apostolate is to be found in a deeper understanding of our relations as
Christians with the natural world and environment in which we
have to live our lives. But here I will pass very briefly over this
because it was largely the theme of the book to which I have
just referred.

It is sufficient here to recall the truth that for us, first, as
creatures of God, and, second, as members of the Incarnate
Christ prolonged in time and space in the Mystical Body, the
natural order is God's handiwork, an expression of His creative
bounty. He made it good—an earthly paradise. And when
through free man's rebellion against Him, the natural world
seemed to become stained with man's corruption, He proclaimed its inner goodness by taking human flesh from it and
thus stamping it with the hall-mark of the divinity.

This seems to be an obvious truth, but it is not an easy one
for man to accept. The reason is that we find it hard to distinguish between man's sin, which is correlative to his freedom,
and the innocence, indeed the divinized quality, of nature so
fully revealed to us in the Incarnation of God. We are tempted
to impute our corruption to nature. And it is true that since
the Fall man has been called upon, hand in hand with the
Incarnate God, to *order* nature, by using it properly, so that in
it may be realized the Kingdom of God through grace.

The task of ordering nature to its supernatural end involves
sacrifice, knowledge and rule which Christians must exercise
with Christ as priests, teachers and kings. We have to sacrifice
a lesser good to a higher good; we have to witness to the right
order which directs what must die and what must live; we have
to see that this is done. But, faced in practice with the difficulty
of the job, we are tempted to deform nature in the interests of

the end we pursue. For example, it often seems easier to escape from nature in order to avoid the suffering of trying to control it. We turn in on ourselves; we live in ivory towers; we think it is enough to carve within a Church distinct from the world a protected path to our goal. We like to forget that Christ is going to come back to judge the *whole* world and all people in their relation to the whole world, to divide good from evil on a spectacular scale, and that this general judgment governs the private judgment which we prefer to think of because it seems to concentrate on us individually and the little world which we have so largely made for ourselves.

One reason for this temptation to escapism is connected with a misunderstanding of the clerical, and especially the technically "religious", vocation. Priests and monks, we know by Revelation, are called upon in varying degrees to renounce the world and the flesh, not merely in the sense in which we all must, namely in so far as they are wrongly used, but even in their right and otherwise necessary use. This is because they have been set apart to follow a vocation of such primary importance in the supernatural order that it demands a specialized concentration. Celibacy, like obedience and poverty, is the subject of a special vow for the special dedication to God in the technically "religious" sense. So valuable and important is this dedication to a life of prayer and renunciation that those who live "virgins" for God's sake achieve a higher state in God's eyes than those who marry. But, apart from this, the way of the spiritual life is to use rightly, not to deny, the things of the world. "Using rightly" involves, of course, selection, and selection means choosing one thing and denying oneself another. Denial, therefore, necessarily enters into right use, but denial for denial's sake and denial in order merely to please oneself, for example in order to enjoy the feeling of being better, purer, more refined and ascetic than others, are not the Christian way of life. Unfortunately, as we have seen, during long periods of history the almost unchallenged influence of clerical and especially monastic spirituality, as applicable to all who had any interest at all in rising above the minimum spiritual conditions of Christian living, led to the view that the nearer the layman got to the cloister and the celibate life, the nearer he got to God. It is only relatively recently, for example, that the canonization of laymen as laymen and laywomen as laywomen became normal. Priests, monks and warrior kings and princes were canonized—the latter as defenders of Christendom—and so were virgins, widows and widowers, especially if they entered religious life after the death of their married partners. The saintly example of married people as married people and of people in the world achieving their spiritual life in the world as, for example, school-teachers, doctors, lawyers, social-workers, is something new, simply because the accidents of history have drawn attention to the growing Christian importance of the laity's rôle. And to-day, when persecution reigns in so many lands, we are back again to early Christian times when the supreme priestly sacrifice (in the spiritual rather than sacramental sense) of martyrdom is a witness of heroic sanctity, clear of all reference to clerical or lay status.

A lay spirituality must therefore be essentially one of courageously facing responsibilities and choosing the way of God's pattern, God's Kingdom, from within the very texture of the world.

The point has been seized in certain simple instances, for example in family life. Much, too, has been made by certain writers of the virtues of agricultural life and the use of rightly distributed property. Working on the soil seems particularly creative and innocent. One's life is regulated by the seasons' rhythm and it is not very easy to do any harm or commit a sin in planting a cabbage. The use of possessions directly related to one's work and family life is also an easy concept, and one into which God fits easily. But any too great insistence on the Christian virtues in such conditions may well betray the same old harking back to a cloistered virtue, the same desire to escape the spiritual responsibilities of lay life.

We have to take the world as we find it, and especially as it may most need the leaven of the Christian spiritual life. The world of technology, of the machine, the world of big industry, of modern administration, the world of secularism and paganism, these are, for the great majority in the West, the world in which God has placed us. It is right that we, guided by Catholic authority, should judge objectively of what in this world can be saved and what must die, but we must resist any temptation to judge these things in terms of our personal spiritual convenience and comfort. Faith, hope and charity are the virtues to be exercised in the midst of the Christian battlefield, and to be exercised with great courage. The more "religiously" unpromising the situation, the greater the lay spiritual opportunity of being priest, teacher and king with Christ. If such an ideal makes us nervous, it is because the laity has not been trained to live up to it.

The difficulty, no doubt, arises from the devout person's sense that in this rough Christian calling of our time, there seems to be no time for prayer, for retreat, for gathering our soul together, for all the things we associate with the spiritual life. I have even heard a priest busied from morning till night with heavy parish work undertaken with a completely selfless zeal saying: "I am all washed up. I am empty. I have no spiritual life left." But surely he was confusing the appearance, the feeling, with the reality. His was in fact the life, under obedience, of a saint, but because he could not say his prayers as he would have liked to and had not time to recollect himself satisfactorily in God, he thought his spiritual life had been killed. Can we escape the truth that if a man lives "another Christ", the grace, the life of Christ is pouring through him, however spiritually uncomfortable he feels?

This is even truer of the layman since he was never called to the sacramental priesthood and service of the Church and is not normally called to the life of prayer in the sense of the life-apart of contemplation. His call is precisely to the active life of witnessing to Christ and from Christ whose life he shares as a Christian in sacrifice, example and—if we may use the word— agency. Once he grasps the supernatural, the divine, quality of the springs from which his spiritual-active life is nourished, his life, properly lived, *is* his praise and service of God. It *is* his prayer and his union with Christ. In a more literal sense, perhaps, than St Benedict, for his monks "to work", for him, "is his prayer".

If I may refer back again to my previous book, I have tried to show in its pages how a firm grasp of the intimacy of our relation to God—God who is "Isness" and nearer to us than we are to ourselves, because He is Reality—and of our unity with Christ in the Mystical Body, makes us realize the spiritual meaning and orientation of all our actions, even if we cannot consciously in the stress and distraction of living always advert to God and Our Lord. Indeed, the gift of devoutness, of prayer in the ordinary sense, of active consciousness of God, appears to be very variously granted to people. Furthermore, it is obvious that the degree in which we can consciously attend to the supernatural must vary with the conditions of our life. That indeed is why so many are set apart in religious orders in order to make a speciality of prayer. That is why the making of retreats is recommended so that we may from time to time take spiritual stock of ourselves and concentrate on devotion. Far more necessary is it that our spirits (and often bodies) be spiritually re-nourished by Mass and the Sacraments. But this does not alter the fact that our job in life, performed for the right reasons and in a Christian light within the limits of our opportunity, *is* our praise and service and love of God. It is, moreover, the test of the reality and sincerity of our devotion. If we cannot all have the same potentiality and opportunity and taste for that devotion as devotion, we nevertheless cannot escape the fact that we must all answer for the way our active lives witness to the Christ by whose power they should, for Christians, be lived.

IV

CHRIST IN PERSONAL RELATIONS

I. PARENTS AND CHILDREN

THE first school of lay spirituality is the family—the family into which we are born and the family which we found when we receive the sacrament of matrimony and bring our own children into the world. About the Christian family much has been written—and written better than I can write. Here there has been no lack of understanding of the special quality of lay spirituality. I will therefore be content with only a few observations.

First, let us note that marriage is correlative to Holy Orders in the sense that both are sacraments, and indeed the only sacraments that directly differentiate and govern vocations in life. It is true that it is not intrinsically impossible to receive both these sacraments, but neither in the Western Church nor in the Eastern may an ordained priest be married, though in the Eastern a married person may be ordained. Ordination after marriage has ended through the death of the wife is not a case of being both married and ordained.

This Church discipline effectively distinguishes two vocations governed by two sacraments. Thus both of these special vocations (marriage may well be considered normal for those not called to celibacy by a religious vocation) attach us outwardly or visibly to Christ in a special manner, and that outward attachment in linked with the special inner attachment to Christ the Priest, Christ the Prophet and Christ the King.

This means that marriage in itself and all that flows from it is a Christ-thing, a state of union or prayer, over and above other aspects of our lives. Christ is with us in marriage and in the family in an extra way that sanctifies our married and family acts, just as He is in us in an extra way in Penance or Holy Communion or Extreme Unction.

Marriage is readily thought of in terms of pleasure, comfort, companionship, but these in fact cannot be separated from the elements of sacrifice, authority and responsibility which true married life entails. Our focus in this matter tends to be distorted by the physical side of marriage which is associated with all that the word "sex" means to our generation. But whereas sex in its usual meaning is something detached, in marriage it is attached to a whole vocation, to a family, and it is attached to the whole supernatural world centred in Christ.

This does not depreciate nor does it exaggerate the place of sex, for once again we must not think in terms of "either, or" (either sex, or marriage), but of enrichments of different elements when they function within the whole. Sex in marriage is glorified by marriage and by Christ, just as marriage cannot be without sex. While speaking of this matter, we can even go further and say that there is really no sex outside marriage: there are only detached acts of sex striving vainly to hang on to an artificial, evanescent little world of man's creation, and therefore wrong. The difficulty, of course, arises from the fact that every person biologically can marry, and therefore every person feels or can feel all that goes with the sexual instinct. Moreover that instinct is pervasive in our whole make-up so that it must in some way affect us at all levels of our personality. But it can only find its proper meaning in relation to marriage or to expectation of marriage or to the relationships of friendship and affection without which marriage would not be possible and which can express themselves in a different way in all ordered human society.

All this is important because it lies at the basis, not only of marriage itself, but of the vitally important sexual education of children and also of the whole subject of what constitutes Christian modesty. Only if we realize that sex is something vital and beautiful in man, yet that this vitality and beauty can only find their full expression, *i.e.* without distortion, in marriage and all that is related to marriage, can we get our principles clear. Marriage grows out of the world of truly personal relations, and sex in its secondary characteristics affects all those relations. Personal attraction, the beauty of the human body, friendship, love, gentleness of manners, all these are good, save when they are used to promote the detached act of sex and passing union. Marriage demands personal courtship, and consequently a particular interest at a particular time (for which proper preparations should be made by good sexual education by parents) in the other sex. But, again, that interest should be directed by the aim, and should stop short of what would be the destruction of the aim. Sex finds its full function only in marriage, but it is a personal and intimate function for the partners alone and a function which must not be in contradiction with the primary function of marriage which is to produce children, new members at baptism of Christ's Mystical Body. Christian modesty is not truly protected by mere social conventions, still less by fear of the life and body which God made for us. It is only protected by a right understanding of the place and purpose of Christian marriage as the true fulfilment of sex which nevertheless rightly expresses itself in a secondary manner in all affection, in chivalry, and courtesy, in vitality and love of beauty.

All this would be clear enough if society were Christian. This does not mean that all would be right, since the temptations of sex are especially strong in men and women thus so completely disposed to the use of sex and all that leads to it. But the difference between the rights and wrongs would be clear. Unfortunately, just as at one time conditions of Christendom led to an undue repression of sex outside a necessarily tolerated use in marriage, with a good deal of depravity "under the counter", so to-day the general loss of the Christian meaning of marriage has led to sex being looked upon as a function with rights and wrongs of its own, apart from marriage. Through this error it becomes attached to many false worlds of its own creation, of a greater or lesser degree of seriousness and perversity, and this in turn must necessarily lead to psychological deformations and more uncontrolled appetites and miseries. Thus this great gift of God, with all the happiness it was meant to give in its right use and setting, leads in fact to frustrations and miseries from which escape is hard simply because the appetite in itself is strong. And how much truer all this is seen to be when we realize that the sacramental character of marriage creates its own proper world, the world of the family and the world of personal human relations, specially stamped with the grace and presence of Christ and His Church. The home itself may well be said to be a church, not in the sense of imitating the ecclesiastical sanctuary, but in its being a sanctuary suffused by the presence of Christ in a different way.

We have seen that marriage involves sacrifice as well as its reward in love and companionship—spiritual priestly sacrifice to God in the Christian home. It involves, too, teaching and inspiration in the mutual support in life of husband and wife where the differences between the sexes complement one another in their different ways of looking at things, of feeling, of understanding in things both spiritual and temporal. Teaching and inspiration are no less needed in the formative and critical years of early childhood where whole lives can be made or marred. The earliest years of religious teaching and first practice of prayer, with its beautiful bringing out of the latent love of God in young children's hearts, constitute for both parents, though at that age perhaps chiefly for the mother, a spiritual responsibility which no priest, however highly commissioned, can supplant, for the inspiration comes from the intimacy of the relationship between parents and child. Let that responsibility be neglected and no subsequent efforts can ever fully repair the loss. Here surely parents are as closely bound as any member of Christ can ever be with the prophetic and teaching power of Christ. Indeed, it is a solemn thought that neither Pope, nor bishops, nor priests, nor layfolk, could be what they are, but in the light of the vital influences to which they were subject at the hands of their parents in their earliest years. One trembles, looking back, to think with what casualness so sacred a rôle was played in one's own life. But this rôle of teacher is not confined to religion. The child has to be brought up to be a good and effective man or woman, and to find in his or her particular goodness and effectiveness the full Christian way as it affects temporal as well as spiritual matters. This part of the upbringing, again because no one can fully supplant the inspiration of the parents, is no less directly connected with the teaching rôle and grace of Christ.

Then there is authority. I will not enter into the somewhat controversial matter of precedence of authority as between husband and wife, father and mother. The point is that we have here a solid example of true lay authority bound up with the kingly rôle of Christ. The authority of parents over their children, especially in their earlier years, recalls the Old Testament authority of the patriarchs which prefigured that of Christ and the Church, and though that authority in spiritual matters is subject to the authority of the hierarchical Church, the Church itself is the first to insist on the parents' unique and irreplaceable rôle. By natural law, by the teaching of the Church and by incorporation with Christ the King, the parent exercises authoritative rights and responsibilities that are unique. Though

D

both the Church and society, rightly protecting the spiritual and temporal interests of the child, who is just as much of an "end in himself" as the parents, must safeguard the child against misuse of his parents' rights and powers, parental authority so long as it is justly exercised stands on its own within the fellowship of Christ.

This is a truth which can too easily be overlooked for utilitarian reasons. We need not speak here of the State's persistent attempts to usurp parental authority in the interests of what it calls good citizenship. But there is the danger also of the priest attempting to enforce short-cuts towards the more efficient religious upbringing and practice of the child over the heads of the parents. All this presents a difficult and delicate problem best resolved by good-will and understanding all round, but it is well to remember that the authority of the parents is always a reality and that it is accompanied with a sacramental "grace of state" whose exercise, even if it seems clumsy and slow, may well produce more solid and lasting results than any ecclesiastical utilitarianism and tidiness.

Unfortunately, as things too often are, the failure of Christian parents to understand the sacred and spiritual nature of their vocation forces on both Church and society emergency measures. But the solution to the problem is not in making precedents of those emergency measures, but in teaching parents the high nature of their vocation within the Kingdom of Christ whose royal authority they share here in a very special way. God willed it so.

Even with good parents to-day there is a tendency to misunderstand the whole position. Piety suggests devotional practices within the home, for example the Rosary recited in common, but it does not suggest to parents—and therefore children themselves do not learn—that even more important than devotions in common is the Christian responsibility for self-dedication to the children on the parents' part, the Christian responsibility for the right upbringing of the children and exercising due authority over them, and the Christian duty of docility and obedience on the children's part. The failure, moreover, to appreciate how all this springs directly from this special sacramental incorporation in Christ, thus of its nature being a prayer and Christian living, tempts parents to evade their own responsibilities by trying to pass them on to the priest or teacher. Devotion and piety in the home are necessary, indeed, as is still more necessary the closeness of relationship between the home and the parish church, where the Blessed Sacrament is present and the sacraments are received, but these spiritual and supernatural enrichments should strengthen the sacramental quality and order *of the home*, instead of being thought of as an alternative or substitute for the latter. Though we can well do both, it is much easier to say the Rosary in common than it is to live the practical love and selflessness, between parents and between parents and children, that are the test of a Christian home. The family that stays together in mutual love and respect is a family that prays together.

Here, perhaps more clearly than anywhere else, we can appreciate the enormous loss to the Church and society of a general failure to grasp what specific lay spirituality means. A proper Christian understanding of marriage and parenthood as a unique and very direct expression of Christ's priesthood, kingliness and inspiration at work within the family, which thus becomes a lay or secular school of Christ in its own right within the Church, would create a new Christian people. Such a people would be trained from the first in the little cell or world of the family, preparing for life in the great world, to be witnesses for Christ and the Church in that great world, and, as witnesses, apostles finding in their living apostolate the school of their own sanctity.

2. "IN LOCO PARENTIS"

Under this same heading, we may well include the rôle of the teacher who replaces the parents in all that part of education which is beyond the competence of the parents or the opportunities and time at their disposal.

There is no doubt that the Catholic teacher has assumed a vocation that is most closely related to Christ's supernatural action in the world in His Church. This is so in the first place because the teacher *is* the delegate of the parents' authority and responsibilities. It is so because the teacher in many respects acts as the delegate of the hierarchical Church, especially in religious instruction and moral upbringing of the children entrusted to his or her care. It is so, lastly, because the teacher can have great influence in shaping the whole Christian life of pupils, whether for the priestly vocation or for a career in the world.

It is impossible to regard such a vocation as just a job, and it is indeed appropriate that so much of Catholic teaching is in the hands of priests and religious who are dedicated, even by vows, to this work. But the teacher's authority, except where it falls directly under that of the hierarchical Church or is justly regulated by the State, does derive from the authority of the parents, so long as the child is subject to that authority. And higher education must be based on the self-authority of the person who seeks such education. The danger is that this truth can too readily be overlooked—by secular teachers just doing a job or replacing loyalty to parents by loyalty to school or profession; by religious teachers replacing loyalty to parents by loyalty to school or religious order or the Church, ecclesiastically understood.

It is true that most parents make few demands, and it is true that schools are entities of their own which cannot be successfully run if parents are constantly interfering. But apart from taking the trouble at least to recognize parental authority when parents wish to exercise it, there is such a thing as remembering its existence, presuming what it ought to be and indeed helping to stimulate and educate it for the good of the Church and the world.

In day and local schools, at least, relations between teachers and parents can be regular, and here it may often be possible for the teacher to help the parents to be more truly Christian parents even if this in the long run means more trouble and work for them. The education of parents in the world as it is may sometimes be more profitable than the education of the children, and in the end ensure a deeper education for the children than teachers, divorced from indifferent parents, can alone give. The true delegation of Christian parental authority, especially if it be ignorant or inefficient, would also seem to demand a Christian influence on pupils so that they learn to think of life in higher terms than merely money-making or making a worldly success, just as it imposes the duty of stimulating proper ambition where this is wanting. Such work as this, where the circumstances demand it, becomes virtually parents' work, and the Catholic teacher, in virtually replacing negligent parents, almost becomes a parent with the graces and status of the parent. The realization of such Christian duties must also lead to caution and criticism about school traditions and professional pedagogical interests where these seem to conflict with the true interest of the Christian pupil.

In boarding schools run by religious, it is to be expected that much prayer and thought will be given to these matters, but because such schools tend to become centres of strong school loyalties and even rivalries, it is possible to sacrifice the real interest of the child to the traditions and success of the school. The fact that the school is a Catholic school, rooted perhaps in Catholic history or closely associated with a great Catholic Order, may disguise the wrongness of sacrificing the unique and individual free Catholic person to the repute of Church or school. But in the past, at least, there has been a more subtle danger, and one closely connected with the argument of this book. It is that the child's spiritual upbringing and training in the school should be governed by the monastic or religious spirituality of the teachers rather than by the child's coming Christian vocation in the world. I do not refer to any attempt to force a religious or priestly vocation on pupils because I am sure that nowadays this is very rarely consciously done. It is even possible that the danger may lie the other way round. In order not to give any impression of doing so, it is possible that true priestly or religious vocations may not be "brought out" by religious and nuns.

No one wishes to go on record as saying that there can be too much devotion, religious service, sermons, retreats in a Catholic school, yet it is surely true that unless these are intimately related with the whole Christian formation of the child for Catholic lay life, their effect may well prove to be double-edged. They may lead to false and shallow piety and in the end to disgust. At any rate, it must be true to say that the first priority, subject to normal Catholic piety and religious practice and teaching, is training for a life whose spiritual test will be the way in which it witnesses in the world to the whole order of the Kingdom of Christ within secular and temporal affairs. Therefore one should perhaps draw the moral that it is not so much the excess of piety and religious training that may be questioned as its nature. If our children can be taught in our schools, as in our families and in our parishes, how true Christian life is always an inner life with God, the Reality of things, and how it finds its true expression in union with Christ and His members in the Mystical Body so that all we legitimately do possesses a supernatural, a Christlike, character, and is therefore an act of religion, there will be much less danger of either apeing or envying the priest or nun among the naturally pious few or disgust with superficial piety among the many. The personal example of teachers, especially when "off duty", is a vital factor in achieving this.

It is not hard, then, to see how the proper Catholic upbringing of children is a matter for parent, priest and teacher in relationship with Church and State. The doctrinal and judicial authority of Christ through the ecclesiastical hierarchy governs and defines the religious and moral teaching the child must receive. Indirectly, it commissions parents and teachers to act for it in these matters in relation with the priest who is directly responsible for parents and children as part of his flock. Society, through the State, must enforce such just temporal conditions as it sees to be necessary to protect children against abuse and to ensure a sufficient education. But at the centre of it all lies the family which directly derives its responsibilities from the natural law of God and its sacramental and spiritual relationship within the fellowship of members of Christ in the Mystical Body. The family, moreover, in its full family life, lived as well as it is able and deriving grace from its membership of the Mystical Body and its special status in it, *is* the worship, love and service of God and thus a necessary means towards the achievement of His Kingdom.

3. CHRISTIAN NEIGHBOURLINESS

We may also speak here very briefly of those wider personal relations between different families, friends, co-workers and indeed all with whom we may come into neighbourly and personal contact. For though such relationships extend well beyond the family, we grow into them from our family upbringing and through them we meet and get to know other families. In simpler and more Christian ages social relations, of which we will speak in a later chapter, grew out of these personal relationships. The latter were more dependent then than they are to-day on living in the same neighbourhood which developed its own community life. From these, wider forms of community grew. To-day, unfortunately, the position has been reversed. Our social relationships are to a large extent created by the complex forms of State administration and the demands of technological and capitalist or socialist industry. But Christian personal relationships should still have a life of their own.

The parish at least should form a real Christian community for those who live in it, though in fact it rarely does. It is a parish of families and neighbours, and one wonders how far the time and work devoted to providing extra religious facilities to minorities of the more devout could not in part at least be directed towards promoting neighbourliness, mutual help, the care of the sick and old, and Christian co-operation with local authorities for the better provision of local needs. In all this, if not in the actual responsibility for the parish finances, the laity could play a responsible, active and useful part.

But beyond the parish in these days especially most of us have personal ties whether with fellow Catholics or with others. Once upon a time, such things as hospitality, charity and mutual support of all kinds among neighbours, relations, friends, as well as towards the stranger who comes our way, were looked upon as Christian virtues in a special manner. Indeed they were characteristic of Christian ages. Nor is this surprising, for they are obvious expressions of the fellowship of Christians in Christ and of the witness to Christ in places or with people where His kingdom is not recognized or understood. To-day, society has become atomized. Families can be neighbours for years and never know one another. Individuals in a great city may scarcely know another soul save in the artificial relationship of the office and workshop or of synthetic clubs and societies. The evil has penetrated right into the Christian community, for many are the reports of new parishioners never being able to get to know their fellow Catholics, and even converts, for whom there should be a special interest and welcome, can live for many years scarcely knowing a single member of the spiritual fellowship of Christ into which they have been received. The present writer is well aware that he himself is as bad as anyone in all this and very much worse than many. Years of class conscious and individualist upbringing in our social manners make it almost impossible to speak to anyone without an introduction, and one can grow to feeling a positive distaste for even our fellow Catholics in the mass.

That generations of social conditioning of this kind should have led to this only proves how completely we have lost the sense of Christian fellowship which should naturally spring from our faith. While perhaps we renew efforts to be more individually faithful and devout, our life in so many ways is a contradiction of all that the liturgy, prayer, Christian doctrine should bring into being almost spontaneously. Yet much of the Christian way of neighbourliness and friendship could easily be revived, especially in parish life, for I myself have noticed that when introductions have been properly effected or some meeting has been intelligently organized and carried out, Catholics find in one another real friends and neighbours.

In this the clergy could certainly do a great deal more to help and promote a new and more Christian feeling. Though they may not have realized the fact, a common faith, common values in the things that really matter in life, common views and interests, do establish a basis on which the relation of love and friendship can easily be built up. But this is immensely strengthened and deepened when it is more fully realized that this friendship is not a natural and convenient relationship but a real, factual inner unity in Christ whose truth and love we are expressing in this pleasant neighbourliness. It is a direct form, and a very important one, of Christian religious life. How important it is can be understood when we appreciate the fact that its loss accounts in large measure for the individualistic and impersonal form of modern society, just as the lack of this Christian unity between countries is at the root of the divisions and wars of the modern world. One wonders, for example, how many Catholics have been lost to Communism, especially from Africa, just because no Catholic bothered to be a friend to them when they came to Europe to study in Western universities.

V

CHRIST IN THE WORLD

I. INTERNATIONAL RELATIONS

THIS last reflection brings us naturally to the subject of social and international relations where the Catholic finds it difficult indeed to be at home, for the simple reason that these relations have become an inversion of the whole Christian order.

Christianity is an international or supranational fellowship, not in any metaphorical or religious doctrinal sense, but in reality. For the Christian cannot be a person with one leg in the Church and the other out of it, though that is how we mostly feel. The kingdom of Christ, and therefore the fellowship of its members, is all-inclusive in all senses of the word. It is a unity in Christ of all Catholics, irrespective of their temporal divisions and functions. It is a spiritual unity of Catholics and those non-Catholics who in God's eyes are invincibly ignorant of His revelation or full revelation and yet whose life is such that, were they to know the truth, they would wish to accept it, for such people would have the baptism of desire by God's grace given outside the normal channel of the Church's sacraments. It is a unity of Catholics and the whole human population because all human beings constitute the apostolic field of the Christian, and Christ's kingdom will not be achieved in this earth of fallen, free, men until what is good is divided from bad and all that is good finds its ordered place in the Kingdom of Christ on earth. It is a unity of all Catholics in the sense that the whole life of every Catholic in temporal matters as well as spiritual comes within the ambit of Christianity so that Catholics are one together in secular affairs as they are in spiritual ones, though they may be *also* divided in the sense that differences between them as human beings express themselves in differences of tastes, loyalties, functions and everything that can divide one person from another. Indeed, were it not for those differences, the unity of Catholics would be more of a formula or abstraction than a rich and living reality. God is one, but not in the sense of the number "one" or the concept "one" which abstracts from all differences. God is one in the sense that within Him is contained all reality with its infinite differences and variations. And the unity of Christians in Christ is a unity comprising all the differences between man and man.

Corresponding therefore to the international unity of all Catholics there are all the differences which express themselves in life and create the character and nature of different countries and of different places and interests within each country. So, while we know we are all one and bound together in Christ, we live that oneness to a large extent in the natural relationships we form in life on a scale that an individual person can actually encompass.

In our own family we experience our closest relationships; then with our friends and neighbours who become constituted into parish and village; thence, perhaps, to diocese and province; thence to country. And another true basis of community can be formed according to our vocation and special interests, for the promotion of those interests and the defence of what is justly ours within them.

Thus it is that Christianity instinctively thinks of social relationships as growing from concrete, living communities upwards, each step up being more remote yet necessary for the ordering of the common interests. Only the Church itself in the fullest sense and the State in a lesser way fall outside this movement from below upwards. The Church is directly commissioned by God to teach and defend His revelation, while the supernatural fellowship in Christ of all its members is the immediate touch of God uniting us all in an invisible manner. The State, too, exercises a necessary juridical power over the temporal lives of fallen human beings to preserve what we call law and order.

But in modern social life things work the other way round. Though in fact we still know our neighbours (if we know anyone at all) better than our M.P.s and our top civil servants and the industrial and trade union bosses and the fashionable names in writing, art and entertainment, it is these who dominate personal and local life and who form the subject of our more intelligent conversations. The State, whether constitutionally totalitarian or democratic, is the boss with whom we have no genuine links and for which our vote is a mere abstraction. Meanwhile, those who realize the inhumanity and danger of the system that has developed in our world look for the solution in equally artificial and inhuman international organizations and authorities or to supranational ideologies that once again are the products of abstract thinking and conceptions of man in the mass.

About all this there is little that the Christian can do, but what he could do is none the less valuable. The causes of the inhumanity of modern life are at least as much due to technological factors as to the general loss of Christian faith. Scientific progress, developing rapidly in a world already divided, through the loss of Christian unity, into separate sovereign States, has given to those States the control of the complex means of modern living in an ever more crowded world. The social injustices that were inevitably the accompaniment of this rapid technical advance have brought into existence political parties and organizations on the same scale as the State or wider than it. And new means of communication and channels of mass propaganda, like the modern press, radio and television, have enormously strengthened the authority of those who run our lives from above and conditioned the people to think in terms that are as false to real human living as they are convenient and necessary to those in charge of the system. The system cannot be broken down save in the torrents of blood and chaos of destruction that an atomic war would bring in its trail. Nevertheless the Christian is not wholly impotent in the face of it all.

In the first place, he knows, whatever the appearances may be, that none of all this can touch the reality of the Kingdom of Christ. The Mystical Body of Christ, of which he is a member, endures. The gates of hell cannot prevail against Christ's Church. No state of world disorder and inhumanity can touch the bond that unites us to Christ nor the pattern of true world order which the Holy Spirit inspires.

This truth is perhaps not always rightly realized. We may tend to think of it too selfishly and individually. We may look to it in too much of a "saving our own skins" mentality in the sense that, come what may, we can save our souls.

It is the fellowship or community in Christ which endures, and our own unity with Him is through the Church. When we think of our persecuted brethren behind the Iron Curtain, we should think of them not merely as individuals but as the enduring Church, cut off from the rest of Christ's members in appearance, but as truly and fully members as we are—indeed, in virtue of their priestly sacrifices with and for Christ, more deeply united with Christ. We deeply regret that so many of them are deprived of the Mass and the sacraments and religious instruction, and rightly so, for these in God's plan are the normal means of grace. But Christ in the Mystical Body is greater than the normal means of grace which He ordained, and we cannot doubt that Christ's grace pours into them through the prayers of the whole Church. If there is a lay spirituality at all how alive it must be in the hearts of priests deprived of their ministry and lay people deprived of their sacraments for Christ's sake. Their lives are indeed one long act of sacrifice. They are our spiritual priests in the most outstanding way.

We may perhaps be worried at the thought of those who fail, and still more at the thought of those who have been conditioned by base means to affirm what in their right minds they know to be hateful lies. But can we think of Christ as a narrow, fallible, human judge? The deep reality lies behind such appearances. Christ reads right into the hearts of men far, far deeper than any torture or psychological mechanism can read. Christ judges at the level of full human freedom, and we may trust His judgment which will only condemn when He is denied with full knowledge, deliberation and consent. Those conditions must be rarely fulfilled in the spiritually dark climate which men have perversely and forcibly imposed behind the Iron Curtain.

Nor can we set any bounds to the flow of divine grace. In founding His Church in His own mystical prolongation in time and space, Christ revealed the normal, visible, Christian fellowship through which salvation is given to man. But we cannot forget that He is to come again to achieve the Kingdom and complete the story of human creation, judging finally between good and bad. We can therefore hope that despite the appearances of a disordered and Godless world with so many millions apparently ignorant of Him or against Him, all the good in these spiritually blinded souls is supernaturalized and stored up by His own means to be in the end revealed as part of the glory of His Kingdom. And of what *is* good He alone is final judge.

We should not therefore look at the modern world with narrowed Christian eyes. We must, according to Christ's revelation, discern clearly what objectively is good and right and what evil and false, for these are absolute and final. But the condemnation of evil does not entail the condemnation of men who do such evil. Such judgment is reserved to God, for God alone can judge hearts. Behind the objective evil lie human beings, souls, called as much as we are to be members of Christ. That is why for the Christian the most impossible of conditions still offer a fertile field for Christian prayer and apostolate. To think of only saving our own souls or of retiring, without sufficient reason, to islands of Christian religious comfort, rather than face up to the vocation of sacrifice and witness to Christ in the world, could be the very opposite of Christianity lived.

In the second place, there are numberless ways in which the Christian can strive within his means to re-order a disordered world, and in striving to do this, he will not only be witnessing to Christ and thus living a life of worship and service, but he will be doing more than others can do to cure the ills of the world.

The work the Christian can do will vary enormously according to the position in the world which he holds. But whatever the opportunities and responsibilities may be, let us not make two fairly common mistakes of oversimplification.

In the first place, our job in the world is not primarily a pious job. We have to be spiritually nourished and we have to hope and pray that those with whom we come into contact may be given the grace of faith which is always in God's keeping. But the setting of the specific secular Christian job we have to do lies in between our devotion and our neighbours' conversion. It is a job of witnessing to Christian values and seeking to make them prevail within the world in which we live.

In the second place, we must not try to achieve a *simpliste* spiritual totalitarianism. In the temporal field, as we have seen, all kinds of legitimate diversities and differences exist. Indeed, it is they which make up the diversity and richness which Christ unifies. We work on that solid, varied soil which is human life on this earth, not in terms of abstractions, whether theological or political. Differences of countries, differences of parties, differences of class, differences of interests, tastes and characters, these are all God-intended realities that must be respected. Christianity is not just a religious association exclusive of temporal differences. It is an association of infinitely varied human beings with a secular mission as well as a religious one, though one God, one Christ, one Spirit dominates them both. We do not want differences destroyed. On the contrary, we want them enhanced. But we want them also harmonizing together and serving one another so that they may all serve and sing the praises of the infinitely rich God. There is of course no simple answer, no single formula. Life is not like that. We are but passing agents in a process which we can only a little understand, but we have to witness to the complex truth as best we can, leaving it to God to achieve in His time the realization of it all which will be Himself.

An obvious example is nationalism, in so many ways a curse of our era. The answer to nationalism is neither to by-pass nations by seeking a religious refuge from them—the amount of room in the Vatican City is strictly limited—nor to abolish nations, for these express long-standing differences of history, tradition, needs, loyalties that have in fact developed from even more concrete local needs and differences.

But when national differences and demands are made absolutely sovereign so that they deny the primacy of God's law and the community of human beings, related to one another in so many ways that do not touch on the limited, if all-important, responsibilities of nation-States, then nationalism becomes blasphemy against God's sovereignty and a sin against the human community whose consequences must be told in the tragedy of war and human spiritual and material impoverishment. The duty of the true Christian is to fight against nationalism and yet to promote all that is enriching to the world and to his own countrymen within the national tradition which is his. And in so far as we strive to do these things we sacrifice ourselves with Christ the Priest, we assert His authority as King and we witness to His teaching as Prophet. In other words, the Mystical Body of Christ is at work through us in the world and His Kingdom is being achieved.

It would be out of the question here even to suggest the ways in which Catholics could express in practice and with effect the Christian attitude to nationalism and internationalism according to the political power and influence they may wield. But even on the level of the ordinary man there are practical ways of doing something. Our vote, even in the best-run democracies, counts for little in itself unless there happens to be a Christian party—which may or may not be a good thing.

But much more powerful than a single vote is the way we act, speak and even think.

War time has proved an acid test of Catholicity. Granting that in a just war it is our duty, unless we have our own Christian grounds for conscientious objection,[1] to serve our country, there is no reason why the true Christian should accept the nationalist war propaganda, why he should vilify and calumniate the national enemy, why he should refuse to condemn immoral methods of waging war—the more so in that both of the great wars of our time have shown the close relationship between immoral states of mind and action in war and the tragic consequences in the subsequent peace. It has been little less than a scandal that the fellowship in Christ between Catholics has meant practically nothing even to "good" Catholics in so much of war and international crises. To be able to continue our religious exercises, perhaps with fervour, while indulging in hatred for the persons of our enemies, who for the most part are only carrying out their duty, suggests the feeblest comprehension of what Christianity is. It suggests that we regard it as a private communion with a God shaped in our own image, not as the unity in Christ for the sanctification and salvation of all Christ's members and the achievement of His Kingdom. Such a scandal measures the degree of blindness to even an elementary understanding of Christianity.

In peace time, many opportunities may come our way for supporting the forces that make for real international under-standing and even for building a small element of such under-standing for ourselves. Every Catholic who can make a friend of a Catholic, or indeed a non-Catholic, from abroad, or of a coloured person in this country or by correspondence with one thousands of miles away, is setting a stone in the Christian bridge that must solidly span the world even if the map of the world remains multicoloured. We refer, of course, not to merely casual friendships picked merely by accident and taste, but friendships and understanding to which are added a common Christian consciousness of their significance. Such relationships may well be organized as has been done by *Pax Christi*.

[1] The whole subject of the Church and War is a particularly difficult one which at the present time is the object of much study, especially on the Continent. The fact that it is possible for Catholics to take within certain limits differing views on it, according to their own consciences, exemplifies a point I shall try to make later, particularly in Chapter VII.

2. SOCIAL RELATIONS

What is true of international relationships has its application also to national and social ones. And in the world as it is to-day, the temptation to bitterness and hatred may be even stronger and harder to resist in social relations than in international ones.

The sense of social injustice has grown rapidly in modern times. Technology, whether in the field of war or of peace, has outpaced the ability of man to develop social institutions that can use it in a human way. The speed and universality of publicity have focused the attention of all on the resulting inequalities, injustices and dehumanization. And though the world's conscience has been deeply moved, the wide loss of Christian faith and values has set material well-being and pleasure as an ideal and fostered a degree of envy that has envenomed the great and difficult task of ordering social life so that it can cope with a human use of the new wealth and power.

While in no way attempting to minimize the real social evils of our times, it is well to remember that when life was governed by simple and human means of production against a background of Christian values the real human differences between rich and poor (not destitute) were small. From the economic point of view, to live in a cottage or to live in a castle was essentially the same life of sufficient food, warmth, shelter and security. We can see that even to-day, for it is at least arguable that the happiest human life remains that of a peasant to whom religion is vitally important and who owns his house, plot of land and the means of cultivating it so that he and his children can live free and fed lives.

Modern life can add to this a host of conveniences and gadgets and spectacles, but at a cost which largely destroys the value of the sounder wealth it can offer in means of culture and better scientific and medical knowledge. All we can do is to create new demands and then try to provide the antidotes to the harm they cause. But the brute fact remains that having created the new demands we have signally failed to distribute evenly and humanly the means of realizing them.

Unnecessary great wealth is combined with unnecessary poverty, while rich and poor become ever more and more subjected in everything to the administrative and impersonal control of the State. Denied the deeper values which culture gave to minorities and which religion and tradition gave to the many, the rich become victims of their own dehumanized wealth and the poor the victims of envy of the rich, of their own dehumanized labour and of public officials.

Is it any wonder that classes and parties and the world itself are divided by mass-distributed social hatreds and revendications, by isms and counter-isms which, representing as they do, not the human being, but only his detached passions and pleasures, cannot even form true communities of interests? Yet the truth obviously is that along this line there can never be any solution. The grass on the other side of the hedge always looks greener, and so long as men cannot find stable standards in basic human values they can never find content.

But this setting still remains one within which Christ can work. Christians are free to take sides, even against one another, in political parties and industrial organizations, but they are surely not free to endorse many of the arguments and policies that are current.

Almost universal ridicule has been poured on the "pie in the sky" argument, and it has indeed been usually stated in the wrong way or by the wrong people. For the well-to-do person to preach to the poor man that he will get his reward in heaven to compensate for the way he is being robbed of his rights on earth by the rich is hypocritical cynicism, and there is no foundation whatever for the view that God intended men to have permanently different social stations on earth to which it is their Christian duty to adhere. But these caricatures do not refute the basic truth that, whether we are dealing with the rich or with the poor, happiness and content can only come when we realize that material values are not enough. Yet political and social conflicts are in fact largely based on the assumption that only material values exist, even if these are extended to include cultural values and the development of the human personality and the like.

We have seen—it is in fact at the heart of all that is being argued in these pages—that God in becoming Man touched all material creation with the mark of the divine and that consequently the spiritual life of the Christian must aim at realizing the Kingdom of Christ in this world, as well as the next, in terms of the created things which God had put at man's disposal in the order of time and space, and in terms of which He

E

Himself will come again for judgment. Christianity would therefore deny itself if it disinterested itself from those political and social questions which are concerned with the best temporal ordering of human life together. In Scripture we have endless examples of the deep concern of true religion with the injustices and material misery to which so many men are condemned. These are the result of human pride, power and greed, that is, of sin. But true religion must be equally opposed to the mere transference of pride, power and greed from the few privileged to the many unprivileged, yet this is what materialism is committed to in its social policy, and what Marxism, for example, elevates to a principle and an ideology. Marxist class-war, in claiming to achieve justice, has in fact spread far beyond the range of professed Marxists the belief that man, as man, is entitled to as much as he can grab of what is going by any means available. This, no doubt, is a lesser sin than the rich man's belief that God has endowed him for his own good and the good of the world with what he or his forebears have managed to grab unjustly from the poor, but it is a sin all the same.[1]

Into all this materialism the Christian brings a sane and balanced view that springs from the whole revelation of the Incarnate God. He realizes that all property is held in trust from God to be used for the better ordering of the world so that in the world all men may be materially equipped to serve God with their bodies as well as their souls. That material equipment includes those material things which are necessary if a man is to be secure and free to bring up his family in decent comfort and pride, while he himself, with his wife and family, can give of the best that is in them in their lives on earth.

How this is to be ensured in practice is left to man to work

[1] The deep Christian sense of the value of poverty in imitation of the poverty, lowly secular position and, above all, the destitution of Christ in His passion and death, has led to a mystique of Christian poverty that has become closely associated with the social question in our times, and even with the Marxist championship of the worker and the proletariat. The model of "Christ the Worker" has been widely set before Christianity as a whole. In so far as this is a Christian protest against the injustices of capitalism and colonialism, it is readily understandable. But it surely involves the danger of narrowing Christ's universal mission as well as of interpreting the ideal of Christian poverty in a fundamentally materialist sense. It is a poverty of spirit, hard for both rich and poor to attain, which Christ taught us. We should work to establish conditions of justice and human responsibility rather than indulge in judgments about others, whether relatively rich or relatively poor. This aim seems well expressed in the social ideal put forward by the Christian leaders in Britain during the war, namely that extremes of wealth and poverty should be abolished in modern society.

out for himself. Our technological society demands a complex economic structure in which wealth is distributed for the most part in salaries and wages that are very indirectly related to the production that must be justly shared. This system, with all its disadvantages, should at least give a better guarantee that salaries and wages will cover what any man is entitled to in justice so that he and his family can live properly. When a family works alone to grow or to make goods for sale, it is subject to all the risks of nature and life, so that if things go wrong there is no use in claiming rights in justice. In a simple Christian society, a man's friends and neighbours or the local community would tide him over. But to be dependent on charity, even if it is really justice, demands high Christian qualities if a sense of grievance is not to be nursed. To-day, we are all entitled at least to official State assistance and insurance. It should, moreover, be possible for the wage-earner or the salaried man to be assured from their employers of wages and salaries due to them in justice as human beings and commensurate with the value of their work.

All this is theoretically simple, but it grows complicated when we look at it from the point of view of those responsible for production, whether they be the State itself, the large industrial companies or the individual employer. These have many calls on the money at their disposal. They need money, most of which has to be borrowed from others who have savings to risk in other people's productive enterprises, in order to get production going and keep it going. They need money to pay fair wages. And they expect money for themselves as a reward for the work they do and the risks they take. It is obviously extremely difficult to set priorities in the way this money is distributed. The money due to salary- and wage-earners is an absolute priority, but the money may not be there if an insufficient amount is spent on financing the enterprise, while those who undertake production will not continue to do so if they do not get what they consider sufficient out of it either in the way of profits or returns on the investment of their savings.

Consequently, we have in practice an immense series of claims and counter-claims which express themselves in political and industrial divisions, in parties, trade unions and employers' associations. Too often, the issue is really one of war—force pitted against another force, the force of the united wage-earners threatening to withdraw their labour for a time against the many forces which can deprive the wage-earner of his work, perhaps for months and for years on end. And success one way or another largely depends on conditions of trade which is subject to an immense variety of influences over which no one has any effective control. The existence of this industrial system has forced the State to play an ever greater part in regulating production and distribution in such a way as to avoid unemployment and to aid industry over its problems. It has also forced the State to take care of the human casualties which, with all the good will in the world, are never small in number.

What is the practical Christian rôle in these conditions?

On the one side, many are busied with the attempt to improve the system. Here there is very legitimate division of view. Some believe that the State should own or control much of industry on the presumption that profits at least would not enter so much into the picture. And it is true that in the past the profit system enabled a few to enjoy money and power undoubtedly due in justice to the many. On the other hand, it is often claimed that in a properly organized industrial system the higher the profits, the higher the wages, or *vice versa*, while in many countries the cost of State services involves a degree of taxation that makes the retention of high profits virtually impossible. But the real danger of excessive State ownership certainly lies in the threat it creates of making a virtually property-less life more and more economically dependent on an impersonal and all-powerful State.

Because of this the Popes have put before the modern world social principles more nearly calculated to safeguard the right to property and to ensure its juster distribution; to enable all workers to share in the ownership and management with the employers in industrial enterprises; and to promote generally all ways of bringing capital and labour closer together so that labour becomes more responsible and employers less free to abuse their power. In a word, *personality* should become more and more the factor that really matters in industry.

It would, alas, be naïve to suppose that vocational industrial organization, co-operation, co-partnership and other systems which flow from Papal teaching on this subject could be generally realized in the world as it is, but these ideals, when they cannot actually be put into operation, certainly point towards the attitude which Catholics should adopt as employers, managers and workers, as well as electors in their political rôle. Immediate interests and responsibilities will doubtless vary and different political views will be taken, but in each case they will be consciously directed towards diminishing the force of purely materialist values, with the hatred, envy, pride, quest for power which they generate. They will at least aim at a better understanding between capital and labour, even though this may mean personal sacrifice. Such understanding would accord as much properly rewarded responsibility as possible to the *person*, the *human being*, wherever he may be functioning in industrial relations. And though our object may be misinterpreted, we Christians cannot surely avoid the duty of reminding those over whom we may have authority or influence that the social content and peace we all profess to want cannot be gained if we refuse to link our economic values with less self-regarding moral and spiritual ones through which alone a human being can judge of what ought to be and what therefore is truly good for him. And if this is a duty when others are involved, it is *a fortiori* our duty where we ourselves and our social claims and expectations are involved.

It can very easily be seen how such behaviour, which may be a good deal more effective in the world than we sometimes think, derives directly from the nature of Christianity and the Church. It all really centres on seeing how social relationships depend on the right enhancement of the human personality in association with other human personalities for the true good of each and all.

We were created by God social persons, that is persons whose proper development depends on the proper use of the natural order and proper association with one another. But wellbeing in this world is not enough—indeed it is impossible, because we were created to find our full realization with God and in God's Kingdom. God became Man to repair the breach between mankind and God through abuse of free-will and to carry us in intimate union with Him along the way to the achievement of the proper pattern in His Kingdom. That way was revealed to the Church which is both divine authority and divine fellowship in Christ the Incarnate God, prolonged in the order of time and space. In so far, therefore, as we, supernaturally bound to Christ, live and express Christ in the social order, so important in helping or weakening true human personality, we are leading spiritual lives, lives of service and love of God. The sacrifices that here, perhaps more than anywhere else, we have to make, if we do our duty; the truths we have to teach in spheres where the commissioned teaching Church cannot easily reach; the witness to the right order which we have to give by our lives and example, even though there may be no simple solution; all these in their supernatural quality integrate us with Christ, Priest, Prophet and King. We cannot look upon our secular citizenship, whether in international, national, or social and economic fields, as divorced *at any point* from our Christian responsibility, however costly it may be to our career and influence. This is all the more so in that contemporary history, both international and industrial, has made it so clear that tragedy follows the denial of the love and true humanism which Christ taught. At the same time, it would be wrong to try to foist these Christian responsibilities on to the Pope or the Church, especially with a view to avoiding them "because the Pope has not spoken". The Pope teaches principles, but he cannot take our place or our responsibilities. Life, personal and social, is concrete, and it demands concrete action in specific circumstances. In the light of Christian teaching, it is we who must all the time be the judges and the actors—and in so doing representing the living Christ.

VI

THE CHURCH IS A LIFE

1. "A MORE EXCELLENT WAY"

I HAVE tried in the last two chapters to outline certain very
obvious principles of Catholic lay conduct within the
family and in the general field of personal, social and international relations between Christians and between Christians
and the far greater number, created by God and called into
Christ's Kingdom, yet not visibly united to it. And I have also
sought to show how right Christian conduct in all these matters
is an active participation in Christ, Priest, Prophet and King,
and consequently the way of supernatural love and service of
God, even though wholly temporal in its activity and context.
I have on purpose avoided the obvious problems of conduct
which these matters raise and which are so often a source of
concern with the world when it studies the Christian record and
the Christian claims.

The reason I have avoided them is because they seem to me
to arise precisely because Christians themselves are so generally ignorant about what their Christian call involves—and if
Christians themselves are ignorant about this, how much more
ignorant is the world! Many of these difficulties would automatically disappear if there were a clearer understanding on
both sides about the meaning of the Christian life.

The common view of the Church as only and simply a juridical institution, claiming to be infallible in faith and morals,
suggests that it has the right answer to every problem, and that
Christians, banded together under that authority and guidance,
should be able to give an example of perfect human conduct
and to resolve such perplexities of life as how to live happily in
personal relations in marriage or out of it, in the problems of
the rich and the poor, above all perhaps to-day in showing the
way of avoiding the disaster of war which threatens everything
we mean by civilization In fact, it is obvious that the Church
does none of these things. So non-Christians, however perplexed

themselves, dismiss the Church as being of no real use to them—
it is just another claimant in the crowded field of ideologies,
systems, nostrums—while Christians themselves tend to distinguish between ecclesiastical and set moral matters, where the
Church is all-important to them because it holds the key to
another and better world into which they will enter after this
rather unsatisfactory earthly pilgrimage, and secular responsibilities that have little or no Christian bearing.

It is only when we begin to understand that Christianity is a
life that we can begin to see the answer to the problem. The
Church *is* a hierarchical, juridical institution because God revealed the truth and way of the Christian life and commissioned
men to come after Him who, inspired and protected by the
Holy Spirit, would teach and preserve that truth and way, and
who would be given special sacramental powers to transmit and
replenish the divine sources of supernatural strength which feed
the Christian life. Given that God chose to constitute this
human channel of light, grace and protection, revealing an
hierarchic and sacramental order within and under which
Christians were to live, it is understandable that we should
jump to the conclusion that that visible order of rulers and ruled,
teachers and taught, priests and people, is the whole story about
the Church. But it is this one-sided view of the Church which
accounts for the too common picture of an institutional, detached, official Church and Christianity standing over against
the normal, outer world of secular affairs, and even of a Church
so detached that it is detached from nine-tenths of the human
living of its own members. The Church, when only understood
in this way, is bound to cause disappointment. When the world
gets itself into trouble, it remembers the Church and its claims and
it demands of it a solution to the trouble. If war threatens, the
Pope should be able to stop it—and so even Catholics are sometimes inclined to think. And when the Pope is unable to save
the world by upholding the claims of those who appeal to him,
the Church is thought useless and its claims no more than
pretensions.

But the Church is also a life—the life of its members united
in the Church, the Mystical Body of Christ. And that life is
lived by us, the members of Christ. In His own Self-Revelation
God revealed to men the purpose of their lives and therefore
of their experiences and problems, and He revealed the rules,
flowing from that Self-Revelation, which have to be followed in

order to attain life's purpose and understand its meaning. But
He did not and could not—given the nature of man as He
created Him—pre-solve for him all the problems of his life and
provide him with an individual detailed chart of how he, or
how society, should act in life. To have done this would have
been to frustrate and render useless those very gifts of intelligence, will, freedom, feeling, intuition, perception which make
man what he is, a creature made in the image of God Himself.
But what God did instead in the Incarnation was to give man
a *new life*, a divine life, even in this world, that is shared with
Himself. The natural life of man, which a man must willy nilly
live according to his powers, was raised by the divinity to an
infinitely higher level of life. Man was enabled to live in and
with and from the life of the Christ-God Himself. And that
is what the Church is: a new life of the men who together
form a society in Christ so that they together do no less than
prolong Christ in time and space. Thus together they are
Christ's Mystical Body—His very life interpenetrating and
uniting the lives of those who live in Him. This Body has its
double aspect. First it is an order which speaks, through delegated human mouths, God's revelation and His will. Second it
is the sharing together of the new life—natural life supernaturalized or divinized.

We may wonder why God chose to make the sharing of the
new life subject to the special conditions of sacramental entry
into it and subject to obedience to a visible hierarchy, though this
way clearly relates to God's plan to make Himself a man and
bring "at-one-ment" with the Godhead through a man's
suffering and death, yet also a God's; but, whether we wonder
or not, that is the way He did choose. And we do know from
the universal nature of His mission, proclaimed by Himself,
that no one is excluded from this new life save through his own
fault.

Once then we understand that the Church is the *new life*
of the members of Christ under the conditions that Christ
ordained, we can begin to understand very much better the
real rôle of Christianity and of Christians in the secular world.
Understanding this, it would be preposterous to suppose that
a *life* could be divided into two lives, a life in the Church and a
life in the world. Such a division must kill a living thing. There
can only be differences of functions and varieties within the one
life. Christians face up to human life and its problems in exactly

the same way as others do, but theirs is the life of spiritual free-men, to adapt St Paul's words.[1] It is a life guided as to its values and moving-force by the Revelation of Christ's life, entrusted to the keeping and rule of His hierarchically organized Church and supernaturally energized by membership together of Christ in the Church which is Christ's Mystical Body. We can measure and calculate the visible difference which Christ's Revelation through the Church has made.

Because of it, we know that certain definite things are true which otherwise we would not have known to be true. We know, for example, of the Trinity or of the Real Presence in the Blessed Sacrament. We know, too, that certain things are right and certain things are wrong, for example, in the realm of marriage and sex. But beyond such clear and calculable differences, there is in the life and example of Christ a whole world of spiritual and moral enrichment of what natural reason can tell us. From this we know, for example, of the prime place which love occupies in our relations with God and in our relations with one another. We know that we are *all* sons of the same heavenly Father, and therefore there can be no fundamental human difference between races and colours. We realize the paradox that only by sacrifice of self can we grow into the true self which is our spirit and yet even so God's Spirit rather than ours. We understand that only through forgiveness of our enemies can we help them and ourselves towards the peace and order that comes from God. These truths spoken so uniquely from the lips of Christ on earth remain through time the inspiration of the Mystical Body, and only from its light, grace and strength can we hope to live by them. It is indeed a matter of *living* by them, for they are not just maxims and rules to be exteriorly applied to circumstances; they are a way of fuller life—a more excellent way—which grows and deepens according as our union with Christ grows and deepens. In so far as their spirit suffuses us, so will they produce the miracles of grace which are unpredictable by human planning and calculation even at the highest level of natural reason and goodness.

Nor are they something merely individual for the saint or genius of the spiritual life. They grow and deepen in our sharing together in Christ, for we are members of one another and members together of Christ. Just as we see in the natural order

[1] Galatians 4. 31.

how emotion shared is emotion raised, so in the supernatural
there is increased strength, grace and light in us *together* for
there Christ is in the midst of us.

That is why we should be so conscious of the Church as a
community or fellowship of Christians in Christ with its supernatural life, a life common to all as well as personal to each. The
witness of the Church is not only its doctrine and order and
strength and ritual; it is in the oneness, the unity, of its members; in their example of holiness (another word for oneness
within the character); in the Catholicity or universality of types
and kinds of people they are in their oneness and holiness; and
in their apostolicity, which is a giving out of themselves, or
rather of the Christ in them. Just as natural individual and
social life develops and falls away in the face of changing conditions and the varying insight and character of the human
beings who affect and are affected by these conditions, so we
must expect that the unchanging divinity of Christ and inspiration of His Spirit will be lived in the Church and its members
in this world according to the human and temporal conditions
of finite, earthly, sinful human beings. But however much we
may fail, the Spirit of Christianity and the Christ-power which
flows within it through its members called to "partake of the
Divine nature" remain with their testimony of the love of God
as the key to all human relationship and the achievement of
God's Kingdom, and their grace to live by God's "more
excellent way" if we co-operate with it.

2. CREATIVE VOCATIONS

I have written the above paragraphs partly so that we may
remind ourselves again of the nature of the supernatural link of
Christians with God, and thus avoid slipping away into the
error of thinking that because secular spirituality is secular, it
is somehow merely a better way of secular living; but I have
also written them because I think that they afford the clue we
need to understanding Catholic lay life at a point of the utmost
importance to us all, even if it does not directly affect most of
us. I am thinking of those who possess the gifts of mind and
sensibility that enable them to exercise great influence on the
world through their personalities, their writings, their creative
abilities in the arts and sciences, and to-day perhaps most of all

through the new and powerful channels of publicity, such as radio and television.

This question stimulates endless and, it seems, fruitless debate. Can one differentiate between a Christian way of doing these things and an ordinary way? Is the Christian artist or writer free to follow his inspiration wherever it leads him, confident in the belief that it is God's inspiration? Has the Church in its authoritative capacity any commission to set limits to his work?

It seems to me that the Christian principles we have outlined do help towards solving these problems, while at the same time they warn us that there are no pat and tidy solutions that can be applied automatically.

The Christian writer, artist, teacher is called upon, fully as much as any other Christian, to express Christ in his work, and to do this as priest and witness to the truth and order which Christ revealed. His religion lies thus in his active and creative work. But Christ's Revelation is not confined to the dogma and moral teaching of the hierarchical Church in the sense of being confined to basic dogmas, principles and rules that can be expressed and expounded in a theological text-book. Nor is it confined to authoritative interpretation as though life were a game all of whose variations fell equally under absolute rules. Christianity is a life, as we have seen, and life's principle comes from within its source. That ultimate source is God in His natural revelation immanent in His free creature, made in His own image, and in His supernatural revelation through Christ who has raised His members to live from His own Divinity. Thus, while the Church gives us Christ's own guarantee about the truth and principles which Christ taught, and while it protects and safeguards the order of divine grace and strength, it can only be in our actual Christian living that Christ can, as it were, be applied to the infinite variations and unknowns of personal and social life in an ever-changing environment. In that sense, each of us is or can be a living revelation of Christ to the extent to which our life within the authoritative Church of Christ is permeated by Christ and His Spirit. Thus we become "other Christs".

There is no question here of weakening the rightful authority of the Church. The Church's rulers, commissioned by Christ and inspired by His Spirit, have the duty to protect the faithful, individually and together, from error and evil, and it is the faithful's duty, no matter how eminent or gifted a person

may be, to abide by the Church's decision.[1] In conditions of
Christianity where the faithful in general have very little consciousness of the nature and fullness of *their* Christ-vocation,
as priests, teachers and rulers within their secular lives, it is
likely that the authoritative Church will feel obliged to guide
and protect Christian life, lived as it is within a largely Godless
world, almost continuously.

To such official guidance the faithful look, though this tends
to bring the unfortunate result that they live part of their lives
by reference to ecclesiastical authority, and feel that Christianity has little or no relevance to the rest of their lives where
guidance is not given. This can easily produce the well-known
scandal that Catholics are pious in their "Sunday" lives, and
yet often worse than others in their "weekday" lives.

But if there were a much wider consciousness among the
faithful of the full truth that *all* that we live and do is done
in and with Christ, a living revelation of Christ would slowly
permeate through the secular world. This living revelation
would apply itself, as it were, to the many aspects of creative
living, of practical decisions, that cannot fall within the direct
commission of the authoritative Church. For this further revelation of Christ is through human freedom. It is not automatic
or magical or miraculous. The Christian, impregnated with the
spirit of Christ and His living teaching and nourished on His
grace, has to face and solve the problem, the situation, with his
own human powers. There is no guarantee of infallibility, no
protection against mistakes. If there were, the very quality of
human life would be destroyed. But, instead, there is not only
a contribution to the problem that would be on the right lines,
because on the Christ lines, but there is the witness before the
world of human beings at work determined in their lives and
minds only to accept the highest principles of life and conduct
which the world has ever known. This in itself must operate as

[1] It should be realized that in matters of these kinds the views of individual
bishops may be governed in large measure by their own personal views, by their
upbringing, by the conventions of their times, and so on. No one would dream of
working out a code of moral teaching as applied to the field of literature and art
from the statements of individual prelates through Church history, since such statements would include all kinds of views from a rigorous and narrow extremism to
great breadth. Nevertheless, the bishop in his diocese has the right and duty to
give the moral guidance which he judges to be right, and the Catholic, if he feels
that the guidance is based on misunderstanding or is based on personal narrowness
and prejudice, must at least, it would seem, respect the bishop's spiritual authority
and seek in the judgment the sound and solid moral warning which it will undoubtedly contain, even if its application may be a matter of legitimate dispute.

a leaven within the world. With Christians so living, as indeed
they did live in the early days of the Church, the life of Christianity would flow through the world as its authority to-day
teaches the world.

Only thus, it would seem, can there be a solution to the
dilemmas which so often confront us. The Christian creative
worker, for example, is certainly entitled to insist on the fact that
he must be guided in his creative work by what *he* sees or feels
and by the conditions of his work, and not by the ecclesiastical
rulers. But he omits to add that this can only be really true
within the Christian revelation if his creation is consciously a
witness to Christ, that what he does, says, or makes is, as it
were, a new statement, a new shaping, a new manifestation of
God's revelation in human life.[1] And if he truly sees and realizes this, he will also understand the necessary rôle of the Church
to which he belongs in protecting him and others from error
and evil according to the specific revelation which the Church
guards and teaches. In this the sacrifice and order, inseparable
from the Christian priesthood and rule, find their Christian
expression. In practice, no doubt, individual tensions must
remain, since these are inescapable when we are dealing with
life, but the fuller realization of what is really at issue would
undoubtedly cause these to diminish.

3. PROFESSIONAL VOCATIONS

There is another very important section of Christians who
would not normally be called creative, yet exert more and more
influence in the world in which we live. It is the professional
class of doctors, lawyers, civil servants, producers, technicians,
officers in the armed forces and the police. It is to this class

---

[1] This must not be interpreted in any narrow or merely ecclesiastical way.
Catholic literature and art are far from being confined to work whose purpose is
to moralize or edify. Such work has its proper use and value, but it belongs
essentially to the religious as opposed to the secular field of Christianity. The
Catholic novelist, dramatist, artist, purveyor of entertainment has a right to all
the freedom of subject-matter and treatment which others claim. But if he is truly
Christian, he must surely be conscious of two things. The first is that the fundamental object of his work is to enhance and order the life which God created and
destined for supernatural enrichment, even if this means being aware and making
others aware of life as it is lived and in its disorder. The second is to remember
that evil is contagious. By dwelling on it even with the best intentions, one risks
spreading it. Hence the need for a delicate and conscientious balancing of which
the sincere artist alone can be the judge so far as intention goes, but of which
others may be more impartial judges in the long run.

that we look as a society and as individuals for keeping things running. In a certain sense, their rôle might be said to be very close to God, for the "thing" which they keep running is God's "thing", life, as we know it, personal and ordered together in society. But in another sense, their rôle appears to raise a problem of vocation and spirituality, because the world is at present ordered in a way that falls very far short of a Christian order.

I have been struck by the fact that in this country the pupils of our Catholic public and greater secondary schools tend to become professional men, doctors, lawyers, soldiers, rather than enter more creative careers or interest themselves in the world of politics. The proportion of the former is, of course, always much higher than the latter, for our society needs professional men more and more, and education is geared to produce them and to offer security in life through them. But the proportion of cradle Catholics in the world of the arts in the broadest sense and in political life is certainly below what the percentage of Catholics in the country would warrant. May not one reason for this be that the Catholic, with a strong, defined faith of his own which is largely in opposition to the values of the modern world both in politics and in the arts, tends to play safe and pursue a career with a limited spiritual responsibility? He is ready to help run the world without having to enquire too closely about the direction in which the world is going. He is nervous of careers which help to decide that direction.

In any world, professional men are needed, and the vocation to them is therefore essential, and in some cases its character, for example with doctors and all who help the sick and the poor, has a particularly marked Christian stamp. On the other hand, the ethics of many members of the medical profession and the ethics of the Catholic are in conflict on certain important points, and the time may come when the conflict will widen. Less clearly defined, no doubt, but perhaps even deeper, may be the difference of moral outlook between the modern soldier, especially under conditions of total war, and the Christian outlook. And in certain countries the duty of a civil servant is hardly reconcilable with Christian principles of the equality and intrinsic dignity of the human being as such. However, for the moment these conflicts are not pressing in a free country like Britain whose moral outlook still remains deeply influenced by its Christian social tradition. Even so, there is

something to regret in an attitude of playing safe which may
be the result of Catholic training in our schools.

That training has concentrated on dogmatic and moral
teaching upon a basis of spiritual life which is a modification of
the clerical spiritual life of the teachers, rather than insisting
upon the fellowship and vocation of Christians in the Mystical
Body of Christ at work just as much in the world of secular life
as ·in the world of religious life. Had there been greater em-
phasis on the latter aspect of the Church, there might be more
desire on the part of the pupils to embrace creative and political
careers in which the Catholic clearly faces the challenge either
of dedicating himself to the values and prizes of the secularist
world or to the re-ordering of that world so that it may be more
closely patterned to the revelation of Christ and the achievement of His Kingdom.

It is in this sense that we should surely feel that despite the
relative Christian comfort and congeniality of safe vocations,
for example that of the small farmer or small business-man,
there is to-day a special call to Catholics who have learnt the
meaning of the Mystical Body of Christ and their incorporation
in it at all times and in all their life, to choose the hard and
dangerous vocations at the heart of the secularist world where
their sacrifices and their witness to Christ can be most effective.
Even if they seem to themselves to be failures because their
visible achievement is small or because the conditions in which
they live make a consoling practice of their religion and a nice
sense of spiritual balance in themselves impossible to achieve,
in God's eyes they may have lived fuller Christian lives. Their
spiritual sacrifices may have brought them closer to Christ the
Priest, while their example, where example is most needed, may
have made them better followers of Christ the Teacher and
Christ the King who apparently failed with the world of His
day and yet triumphed in that failure.

4. NO QUICK ANSWERS

Perhaps it is possible for us now to appreciate better that the
great questions which the world puts to the Church, as well as
some of the answers given, rest on a misunderstanding. More
and more, our world seeks for panaceas and grandiose institutions. Some ism will be born to save it; some world-State or
super-international organization will arrange for it peace and

prosperity. It is all part of a general recoil from responsibility and even life itself. But in practice the ideologies and the plannings are ineffective unless they can be allied with political and social tyranny so that mankind is dragged by chains along the way to Utopia. And Utopia grows daily more distant, for it is only in free, responsible *living* that man can work out his salvation personally and as a society.

It is at that level that Christianity makes its impact. If we think of Christianity *only* as an institutional Church, we are in danger of adding another plan, another escape from responsibility, to the world. And, as I do not wish to be misunderstood here, I must add yet again that the institutional Church is vital and primary. It is so because Christ revealed to it the certainties we need for living the Christian life and because He willed that it should be through the sacramental link between the visible order of nature, time and space and the invisible life of Christ prolonged in His Mystical Body that the divine power to achieve God's Kingdom in ourselves and in the world, which He is to come again to judge, flows into us and makes us co-partners with Him. But Christ came to give us life and to give it to us more abundantly, and it is the *life* that transforms society and achieves His Kingdom. That life in every member of Christ, in himself and in community with his fellow members of Christ, is Christ's life which He came to give the world, and we together in Christ, under the authority which He commissioned, form His Mystical Body which is His Church.

It is in the members of His Church living Christ more fully that their lives become more responsible, free and fruitful. And it is the example of such lives which penetrates into society and stimulates more responsible, free and fruitful lives in it.

Being a question of more responsible and better ways of living, there can be no question of sudden transformations, sudden achievements, sudden perpetual peace and justice and order. Life is always a process of growth and decay, of ups and downs, of better and worse, according to how it is lived. Christ gave us the assurance that the gates of hell should not prevail, that He would come again in triumph, that His grace was sufficient for us; but He assured us of no more.

How the world goes depends on how men live, and how men live depends very much on how far Christians live Christ and by Christ's standards for the world as God created it. Nor should we take too narrow a view, as though somehow the visible fellowship of Christ, the Catholic Church, were delivered into a world that is otherwise in complete darkness. Not only has God's revelation been given in part to the human reason, heart and conscience, but Christ came to save *all* men, even the many millions who can never have known Him either in His prefiguring in the Old Testament or in the full revelation of the New. This must mean that He has His own links with all men of good-will who through no fault of theirs are outside the Church He instituted. It must also mean that the Church of God is not unrelated, behind the visible scenes, so to speak, with the long history of man's endeavour to find God, through religion, art, poetry, social institutions, for in these there is something that must live, if much also that must die. The Christian's witness is not in a world that is spiritually dead, but one in many ways predisposed to hear the message of salvation here and hereafter and to receive the grace which super-naturalizes life and enables it to be fruitful because it is the touch of God Himself.

But though God alone can judge the nature of the soil in which the seed is planted, we do know that, as Christians and members of the visible Church and the fellowship of Christ in His Mystical Body, we have a Christ-full life to lead all the time and one which, if human frailty separates us from the Divine, can be forgiven by an all-merciful God responding to an act of love on our part. That Christ-full life of ours, en-lightened by the Holy Spirit and under the specific Revelation and authority committed to the Church, is a very heavy re-sponsibility, for it is meant to be the witness in the world of "the Truth, the Way and the Life" from which so many of our neighbours are cut off in whole or in part, despite the good-will in them.

The Christian witness to the truth, and consequently the world's realization of the value of the Church in answering the deep spiritual and moral dilemmas of life, rests with the insight and example of Christian lives, marked by the "harvest of the spirit", love, joy, peace, patience, kindness, generosity, for-bearance, gentleness, faith, courtesy, temperateness, purity.[1] And these apply to social as well as individual conduct.

[1] Galatians 5. 23.

VII

LAITY AND CLERGY

I. TWO FUNCTIONS

So far I have been trying to draw out the implications of the fellowship of Christians in the Mystical Body of Christ as they affect us, or should affect us, in our secular lives as laymen. Our membership of Christ through grace is not a matter of words or some kind of vague, distant relationship, as though we received some obscure and undefined favour which in practice leaves us very much as we were before. If we are content to think of it in this way, it is because we have grown accustomed to think of ourselves as members, where religious and ecclesiastical subjects are concerned, of an institutional Church that somehow stands between us and a God even more distant and set away from us than the Church.

Our membership of Christ *is* life with Christ—our natural, secular, daily life supernaturalized, that is, revitalized by Christ, so that in living we exercise the Christlike functions of sacrificing, witnessing, ordering, for the achievement of the Kingdom here and hereafter.

And our membership *together* with Christ in the Mystical Body which is the Church is a life together, a living society of sacrifice, witness and order within which we all have different functions, whether of the authority directly delegated by Christ to a chosen number; whether of the sacramental priest-hood through which the Sacrifice of Calvary is perpetuated; or whether of making up the Body of Christ as "other Christs" at all points within that secular society that will be judged by Christ at the last day, as we shall be privately judged when our term of service on earth ends.

Whereas Christ entrusted to the Church the deposit of faith which is essential and unchangeable knowledge for man's guidance and life, and whereas He also revealed the sacramental system of the Church by which the life of Christ is normally mediated to mankind, He did not reveal a *secular* system of dogma or a set of *secular* rules of society, since He intended us to find our way in secular life through the use of those free, responsible powers which make us men created in His own image. Hence there is a clear division between the ecclesiastical sphere and the secular or temporal sphere; but there is no division between the Christ of the hierarchical and sacramental Church and the Christ of the secular world; there is only a difference of action and function. Hence, too, Christ is not divided within us in respect of Church and secular society or in respect of what we call our religious life (our obedience to the hierarchical Church and our liturgical and formal prayer) and what we call our daily life in the world. The Church as the Mystical Body totally covers it all, and our call to be living witnesses to Christ in the world is our Christian job and our way of salvation. We are one with Christ the Priest, Christ the Prophet and Christ the King in so far as our secular life is Him in us revealing His more excellent way.

Just as Christ is King of this world as well as Founder and High Priest and Ruler of His Church which, in one sense, is not co-terminous with the world, so we Christians have to live our Christianity in both a secular and an ecclesiastical world, and this creates a problem that is not always squarely faced in terms of the two aspects of one Christian life.

As I have tried to show, there has been a distinct tendency in ecclesiastical history to see the Christian life as an escape or refuge from the world. For generations of Western history, the Church was called upon to remould society, and, looking back, it seems clear that this was providential, for in the conditions of temporal life then obtaining, there was in fact no other way of establishing what we call Christendom, that is a temporal order moulded in terms of and actuated by Christian principles. But the price that had to be paid was a laity divided into the devout whose spirituality was essentially apart from the world and into the mass who fulfilled (or did not fulfil) their essential religious obligations while living virtually secularist lives. That, together with the dangers inherent in a clerical world with too large a responsibility in secular affairs, caused the division of Christendom and the long period during which the Catholic Church was in open conflict with both Protestantism and secularism. Even so, society evolved within a spiritual and moral mould which it owed to Christendom and reached the free, responsible and educated lay ideal which we know, and indeed are defending, to-day.

It is these conditions which appear to give hope that the right balance between Christian clergy and Christian laity, between clerical or religious spirituality and secular or lay spirituality, can be gradually realized. So much, indeed, of the Church's emphases under recent pontificates point in this direction, not only in the development of Catholic Action but in the trend of liturgical reform. To help, therefore, towards understanding the relationship between the religious and the secular aspect of the layman's Christian life, we shall need to consider briefly both of these subjects.

2. CATHOLIC ACTION AND ITS FULLER IMPLICATIONS

Catholic Action is in itself an extension of the action of hierarchical and juridical Church rather than part of the lay witness to Christ in the world which is the duty of every Catholic as an integral member of Christ's Body; but in effect it goes far to act as a bridge between the ecclesiastical and secular field and it can be a training for secular spirituality in itself.

By definition, Catholic Action is under the ecclesiastical authority of the bishops and its purpose is really to replace the priest by the layman or laywoman in so far as either is canonically capable of so doing. And the need for it has arisen because nowadays it is often impossible or unsuitable for the priest to do the necessary work of evangelizing and teaching in places where these are most needed.

It is in the homes and places of work that are mostly to be found the souls that need to have the Gospel preached to them and to return to the sacraments. And Catholic Action, in fact, started and developed in countries that are nominally Catholic, in other words, in countries where many have been baptized Catholic and perhaps received the sacraments in early youth, only to fall into virtual secularism later. A proportion of such people would resume the practice of their Catholic lives if the priest could come to them. In fact, there are far from enough priests to do this, and too often the priest would be highly unwelcome in the environment in which they live. The only thing to do is to train Catholic laity to go instead of the priest.

The trained Catholic worker in the factory, the trained Catholic helper who can minister to needs within poorer families, the trained Catholic nurse in hospitals—such trained Catholics as these, and many others, find plenty of means of encouraging Catholics to return to their duties and to stimulate the conversion of others by the example of their lives and the application of the techniques in which they are trained.

Work of this kind is necessarily under the direct authority of the hierarchy, for it is an extension of the teaching and pastoral office which normally falls to the clergy and those whom the clergy depute to help them in parochial work. The secular world in this way becomes a kind of parish to which the Church, with lay help, comes with its evangelizing mission that will fill empty churches.

Catholic Action in this form is logically expressing itself in the form of a type of lay religious order called Secular Institutes. In these, unmarried men or women, still living in the world and exercising secular professions, bind themselves with religious promises or vows to pursue a religious spirituality in support of their apostolic action in the world. To ensure this, they devote part of their lives, e.g. their normal holidays, to a form of monastic living in community.

All this is therefore a special adaptation of the monastic and ecclesiastical ideal of religious life for the purpose of extending its influence into the secular world. As such, it has become necessary and invaluable, and from the point of view of the theme of these pages, it underlines the dignity of the lay vocation within the Church. For those who work under formal Catholic Action are directly linked with the canonical authority of the Church that derives from Christ's commission to Peter and the other Apostles. They are members of Christ the Priest, Christ the Prophet and Christ the King, not only as we all are from our membership of the Mystical Body, but also as commissioned from the hierarchical and sacramental Church. They live and witness as extensions or part of that visible authority.

In practice, however, it is not always easy to delimit work that is formally Catholic Action from something that could roughly be called Catholic Activity, and this in non-Catholic countries in particular. In such countries, the people have never been Catholic, so it is not a question of bringing them back to the practice of their faith, but rather of working along lines of remote and indirect conversion. By remote conversion work one means working to restore conditions of society and living more consonant with the spirit of Christ, and in such ways as are available making the Church better known and understood.

This is the task that lies before all Catholics through leading Christ-lives within the world and within their secular avocations and by showing the example of Catholicity as it should be. But there is a tendency to do this by specialized grouping. In Britain, for example, there are many Catholic societies, some of a fairly general nature such as "The Catholic Parents' and Electors' Association" or "The Sword of the Spirit", and others designed to help Catholics in their professions, e.g. doctors' or civil servants' guilds, or to forward a special work, to help the sick or the poor or prisoners, etc. When such societies are formed, they become Catholic social entities on their own, and they formally find their place under ecclesiastical authority. Because, as a formal society, they commit the Church, it is necessary that the Church have direct authority over them and responsibility for them.

But in fact in most cases their work is dual. For example, a society like the "Parents' and Electors' Association" (CPEA or CPA) involves work that is properly secular and work that nearly relates to the juridical Church. For example, the defence of the right of Catholic parents to have their children educated as Catholics is a clear case of something that springs directly from Catholic dogmatic and moral teaching, and there can be no division of opinion about it among Catholics. It is, moreover, so important that the ecclesiastical authority must be responsible for it. But a Catholic parent or a Catholic elector has many social and political interests which *he* believes in because *his* Christian life and values express themselves in a certain opinion, course of action or party allegiance. But his particular views are not necessarily shared by all his fellow Catholics, nor in the personal views of those who exercise Catholic authority. In other words, such matters, though wholly a Christian interest to the true Catholic who realizes his vocation to be a witness to the Christ-life in everything he does, are not directly under the authority of the Church. And this may well be the case even when, in certain matters, most Catholics, clerical and lay, may be in agreement on a social or political line. Even in this case, the very best of Catholics may legitimately have a different view from a majority view which looks like a Catholic view.

There would seem, therefore, to be no reason why Catholics should not form Catholic societies, either in some respects subject to the hierarchy and in others not, or wholly lay and independent, save for the overriding authority of the Church where faith and morals are directly and clearly involved.

The position of a Catholic newspaper in Britain is interesting in this context. Our newspapers are, of course, subject to hierarchical authority in faith and morals, matters which in fact might well be constantly touched upon in the course of reporting news and expressing Catholic views about it. This truth is well in the mind of those responsible for the newspapers. But in practice these newspapers, independently owned by laymen, only very rarely receive direction from the hierarchy and rarely need to refer to ecclesiastical authorities save to get Catholic news and Catholic views as part of their journalistic job. The reason, of course, is that those who own such newspapers make sure that those who work them are responsible and knowledgeable Catholics with a clear idea of where Catholic views may differ and where they must be the same.

In this example we surely have a model of much of that territory which involves both ecclesiastical and secular matters. In practice, however, the tendency has been to see the whole work of a "mixed" Catholic society as being subject to the ecclesiastical authority, even though verbal encouragement may be given to the lay members to "think for themselves". The result is that so many Catholic societies are ineffective and moribund. This lamentable effect derives quite simply from the truth that effective Christianity must be a living Christianity. It must be a life, and you cannot truly live without exercising freedom and responsibility. Though the hierarchical authority exercises—and exercises in a very special way—the function of teaching and ruling, it cannot substitute itself for the Christian function of *living* Christianity, not only in the religious aspects of Christian living, but in its far more extended secular aspects. The alternative must be to confirm the too common delusion that the Catholic's Christian life does not extend to secular life, save where dogma and the moral law fits itself automatically to a certain state of affairs. Is it altogether unfair to say that as things are a more effective Christian secular witness can be made by the laity outside all clerical organization than within it? Where there might be a most valuable bridge, there is a void.

There is a further delicate topic that arises here. The Church itself obviously has a number of material and secular interests. Its apostolic effectiveness is, moreover, greatly bound up with the authority it possesses in the secular society to which it belongs and with the experience of the ways of that society which it can acquire. At present, all these interests are practically exclusively in the hands of the officers of the Church itself, that is, the clergy. The economy and material needs of the parish are usually administered by the parish priest alone, even though the resources themselves are in whole or large part contributed by the laity, and, whether on the national, diocesan or parish scale, the laity play little or no part in strengthening the hands of the Church in its relations with the civil society, except when they are necessarily asked to carry out the policy of the ecclesiastical authority in central and local government and other spheres where the layman alone wields the necessary power.

It would not be out of the scope and intention of these pages to argue the advantages of decisive changes in this matter from the point of view of greater efficiency of action all round. The well-known Italian Jesuit preacher, Father Lombardi, has put forward suggestions that are far in advance of anything that has been even thought of in Britain or America. He has proposed, for example, a lay Senate in Rome, and representative consultative assemblies at the national, diocesan and parochial level—assemblies through which the work of the different Catholic organizations at each level would be harmonized or superseded.[1] In Britain, the most that has been discussed and to some extent tried in one or two places is a lay organization of the parish for Catholic social action in the district.

But we can study these lines of reform from quite a different angle. Representative lay bodies could promote lay co-operation and responsibility even in matters that have long been entirely clerical, for example the running of the parish finances. As such, they would prove a very valuable way of making the faithful understand what the fellowship of Christians means. For this purpose it may be unnecessary to think in terms of national and diocesan levels, but at the parish level there could be scope for some kind of representative sharing in suitable responsibility and initiatives which would embody the living Church in its double aspect of a divine institution and *a community of all in Christ's Mystical Body.*

[1] See Congar, *op. cit.*, p. 365.

Such sharing should not and cannot be interpreted as any lay sharing in the authority and function of the teaching and ruling Church, but there is surely room for a genuinely responsible and representative sharing in the many secular aspects of ecclesiastical life. Such responsibility would in fact express the elements of "consent" and real, living, co-operation which complete, as it were, the whole life of the Church praying, teaching, ruling and living, in the Body of Christ.

One feels the necessity of stressing responsibility and freedom, under the rule of the Church, because there is always a danger, not wholly unkown in the practice of Catholic Action, of ecclesiastical authority being increased and lay initiative being weakened. Catholic Action, because it involves a better organization of Catholic forces under the bishop, can come to mean that many things previously left to individual lay initiative simply because they were no one's special business now directly depend on episcopal authority. Thus, though Catholic Action was intended to extend the scope of lay initiative and work, it can be so carried into effect as actually to diminish it. The same would obviously be true if a better organization of parish life, through lay co-operation, in effect simply put more real authority and decision in the hands of the parish priest.

As things are, very much depends on the character and outlook of bishop or priest. Under the same organization it is possible to give real scope and responsibility to the layman or to give him nothing but the shadow of them while expecting from him all the donkey work.

On the other hand, one must frankly recognize the intrinsic difficulty of defining in any way a constitution that will genuinely separate responsibilities when, of course, we all gladly accept the Christ-commissioned overriding authority of the hierarchy in all matters of faith and morals. The application of this authority to changing circumstances cannot easily be defined *a priori*, any more than the lay witness to Christ in the conditions of actually living Christ in the world cannot be expressed in any set of regulations.

Indeed, the practical solution in the long run must always greatly depend on the personal Christian qualities of those who exercise ecclesiastical authority and on the education of the faithful to the fuller understanding of what their Christian life and vocation really means. And, in the end, both these depend on the way Christianity is lived and taught in the family, the parish, the school and, for the clergy, in the seminary. It is well to remember that even Popes and bishops were once lay children and lay young men whose Christian outlook was once formed and perhaps set in circumstances exactly similar to those of all the faithful.

3. DEPENDENCE ON THE CLERGY

It would be cowardice on my part if at this point I did not say a word or two about the training of the clergy, even though I know that this is a subject particularly outside the business and competence of a layman. I do so only in strict relation to the theme of these pages.

The spiritual life of the laity must in practice depend almost entirely on the clergy. And the training of the clergy is given in the seminary system. This training which throws together a number of young men in an atmosphere that must still have a good deal of the school or university about it is bound to create something of a class or caste mentality. The normal human growth from the family into which a man is born into the new family made by marriage is broken. Normal personal relationships, developing from a natural society, are altered. How far can the loss be minimized? Undoubtedly, a wise spiritual training is the fundamental answer, and many have noted, whether justly or not, that the longer and deeper training of the religious orders goes far to overcome the difficulty. Here we get the interesting paradox that priests trained in communities sharply cut off from the world find themselves better adapted in the end to help the laity to lead real Christian lives in the world. The *familia* of the religious order has successfully replaced the natural family. But beyond this one wonders how far the subject of spiritual and personal relationship with the faithful is given a priority in the seminary. Spiritual relationship entails the careful study of the Church as a community, a fellowship, in Christ. Personal relationship must depend in the end on breadth of view, on all that is implied in the phrase "liberal education", on a realization of the values, customs, courtesies, understandings that are current in the life of the times and expressed in literature, periodicals, wireless, and so on. Even if much in these has to be condemned, they cannot safely be ignored. May there not be a danger that the seminary which falls short on the one side of the new spiritual family that a great religious order creates and yet is cut off from the natural societies, from family up-wards, of secular life, fall, as it were, between two stools? It is enough to raise the question; it is for others to study the ways of meeting the difficulties.

Certainly we must admit that the development of a fuller and better balanced lay spirituality so much needed in the world to-day will hardly be realized except through the teaching, encouragement and example of the priest—and this truth will be better seen when we consider in the next two chapters the relationship between religious observance and lay Christian life.

VIII

THE PRAYER OF THE LAYMAN

RELIGION is, literally, the link between God and man, and human life only has a meaning in so far as we strive to know, love and serve God in this world and thus to realize God when we are taken away from the order of space and time. This time and space strings out, as it were, our beings so that they can grow, in relation to one another and their environment, and thus realize the quality, the fullness, in their natures which will be timelessly absorbed in God, the really Real.

We have seen that this knowledge, love and service of God is expressed in and through that living in time and space which is our growth, our self-realization. And in the revelation of the Incarnation we have learnt that God Himself became Man in order to share with us the power of the divinity which alone can make any human knowledge, love and service worthy of Him and any self-realization a God-realization. In particular, we have seen that God prolonged Himself in the order of space and time through His Mystical Body which is His Church so that our membership of the Church is a membership of Christ in whose priestly, prophetical and kingly nature we can share. This makes our actual living, if it is lived to the best of our ability and for the right intention, *a continuous act of prayer, worship and service.* This is just as true for the layman, living in the world where human powers of fallible intelligence and feeble will and easily corruptible emotions have to be our practical guide towards the realization of God's Kingdom, as it is true for the contemplative monk or nun whose every action, so far as is humanly possible, is regulated by the supernatural certainties of faith.

But it is, of course, obvious that in so far as we can purify our intentions, substituting God's being and will for our own, we shall be able to know, love and serve God better and realize Him more fully in ourselves. It must be admitted, as a matter of sheer evidence, that the capacity and taste for living close to God varies enormously among human beings—God did not create us intellectually and physically equal, and there is no reason to suppose that He created us religiously equal. The conditions of human living, furthermore, are so disposed as to allow of very different opportunities of prayer and specifically religious service. If we all entered monasteries, we should be manifestly disobeying God's will. And the greater part of our secular activities do not allow, in terms of the spiritual capacities of the vast majority of even good men, of the conscious prayer to God which is attainable in conditions of monastic life for those called to it.

On these points, it seems to me that we ought to be rather more realistic than some preachers and spiritual writers often are. We have fallen natures, and Christ in His life on earth surely showed Himself, if we may so put it, as human as He showed Himself divine. He loved the weak and stretched Himself out to the sinful, while reserving His harshest words for those who gloried in their righteousness and fidelity to the letter of the law. It is really not to be expected that human nature as we know it, in ourselves as much as in others, will be radically changed. But it is to be expected that Christ is ready to help everyone and that His call is for everyone. Indeed in some mysterious way it often looks as though Christ's call can be more readily heard from the depths of sin than from the heights of apparent virtue, no doubt because it is the sense and realization of sin which gives a man of good intention the deepest sense of his own nothingness and misery in separation from God. And we have seen that Christ's helping hand is so powerful and far-reaching that in so far as we do not deliberately reject Him we are, despite our human weaknesses and miseries, rendering Him an acceptable and, indeed, divine service. He has willed it so that, within His Mystical Body, when we are not against Him, we are, though we may hardly realize it, with Him.

Still, none of this can take away from the truth that we must all, as best we can, aim to be "perfect, as your Heavenly Father is perfect" and that our value to God and to the world as Christians greatly depends on how well we fulfil our Christian task. And this, in turn, cannot be divorced from the amount of religion—linking with God—we can sincerely and authentically live. One uses the qualifications "sincerely and authentically" because a good deal of what appears to be religion is not truly religion, but often a subtle form of hypocrisy and worship of self rather than of God, and because, as the whole theme of these pages argues, quantity and quality of "religion", as distinct from "spirituality", need to be carefully related to the very varying vocations of the Christian life as a whole.

It is not for nothing that the Catholic Church lays down minimum regular religious obligations, namely, hearing Mass on Sundays and going to Communion at Easter, together with the laws of fasting and abstinence. Observe those faithfully, keep out of serious sin or repent of it, and you have done your duty. You are still a member of Christ's Mystical Body, and your Christian life, which may well be more edifying than that of many who do much more, is a sharing with Christ, and therefore an acceptable prayer and service. If you fall into serious sin, Our Lord's call is to the great Sacrament of Penance which He instituted to make you a fruitful member again of Himself. Thus, you are practising secular spirituality, and who can say whether this "minimum" may not be the sincere and authentic "maximum" for some very good Christians?

But the Church, though laying down a minimum, constantly exhorts to more and much more. Evidently, the more we can make *God's own* in our religious observance, in the real sense of those words, the better. It is important to underline "God's own", since it is so very easy to make prayer, religious observance and mortification a subtle way of serving ourselves instead of God. Apart from crude pharisaism and hypocrisy, we can so easily take pride in our "spiritual progress" and seek a human comfort in the cosiness of a pious life. Our loyalty may also be given to a certain *bien pensant* Catholic attitude which may be a mixture of snobbery, patting ourselves on the back and looking down on others whose gayer and more natural life we may secretly envy. This is not a subject that can be pursued in these pages, and it is only mentioned as an additional way of suggesting that it is not for us to judge others according to any evidence of their external religious observances. They may prefer to do less, and do it well, than to do more for reasons about whose integrity they are doubtful.

All this, it appears to me, is extraordinarily well suggested in the Church's liturgical prayer, especially when we approach it in terms of the lines of reform—or rather return to earlier uses—which to-day is so much in the mind of the Church.

There is a sense in which liturgical prayer does not seem a prayer at all in the usual meaning of the word. When we think of prayer, we think of the individual person going on his knees and either reading prayers from a prayer book or engaging in a kind of colloquy with God—telling Him his troubles, asking for His help, begging for favours, making acts of affection, and the like. But liturgical prayer, though it includes this, is not really like it.

The liturgy, to begin with, is a public drama centring round Almighty God. Within the cycle of each year and even of each day the theme of the Creation and the divine Incarnation is enacted in a unique fashion. In one sense the story is retold, the various liturgical seasons illustrating and reminding us all of "In the Beginning", the coming of Christ, His birth, life, passion, death, all culminating in His resurrection, the coming of the Holy Spirit, the birth of His Church, and the theme pointing forwards to the return of Christ in triumph for judgment and the achievement of the Kingdom; but in another and much deeper sense the whole of that drama is mystically *lived again* because the central act of the liturgy, the Sacrifice of the Mass, *is* the perpetuation of the Sacrifice of Calvary, while the Church *is* the prolongation of the Incarnation in Christ's Mystical Body inspired by the presence of the Holy Spirit and comforted by the presence of the Eucharistic Christ.

We are not merely actors in a play, but living agents in the reality, mystically relived. By God's power, the symbol, while remaining in appearance symbolic, is also the reality.

When we appreciate this, we begin to realize that the liturgy is more than a prayer in the ordinary sense of the word. In it, we are so integrated with Christ that our being and our actions are mysteriously linked with the being and actions of the Incarnate Christ on earth. Our prayer, from being a human raising up of the mind and heart to God, has been converted quite literally into a way to Almighty God "through Christ and with Christ and in Christ, who lives and reigns in the unity of the Holy Spirit". In liturgical prayer, our presence, our actions, our voice, our singing are a re-enactment of the drama of creation, which is centred on the life of Christ who, through suffering death and resurrection, made us one again with the Eternal Father. Our sharing with Christ in this way causes our prayer immediately to reach the Eternal Father in adoration, praise and service.

That is why so little can effect so much: a few drops of water in the simplest of ceremonies can make us members of Christ; a few words uttered by Christ's accredited minister can bring us forgiveness for the deepest of sins; above all, the short half-hour of the Mass focuses the very heart of God's purpose in creation and brings down from heaven Christ's very Body and Blood.

But two points have to be noted. None of this takes place automatically. We have been created *free* personalities, and our free co-operation in a responsible way is the absolute condition of our sharing in this divine order. Nor is this a gift to us individually as though all that mattered was God and myself. It is through our membership of Christ's Mystical Body, which is the Church, that we can act in this drama and share in the renewed mystical life of Our Lord. We are members of one another in the supernatural order as we are in the natural. These conditions mean that the quality of our intelligence and our will to do what the Church does and to do it with the Church are all-important. The whole liturgy, in its public nature, in the fellowship it supposes, in the significant quality of its actions and in the majestic beauty of its prayers, proclaims these truths. Why else the drama, why else the wonderful linking of the Creation and Incarnation to the seasons of the year and our natural social world, why else our parts in the script, the parts of the faithful, the laity?

We know how very little we need do to share in the great mystery. Scarcely more than a lounging bodily presence near the exit of the church, with the right intention, suffices to secure the infinite benefits of the Mass. And this fact is deeply important because it is in fact the way to salvation and sanctification, and many who perhaps have never really had a chance of understanding the meaning of the Mass except as an obligation are hardly likely to do much more. But as one grows to understand something of the Mass and the liturgy, one must realize how wonderfully it expresses the way Christians can and should intelligently play their part in religion and in life.

In the liturgy we can escape from the haunting worry of our self-conscious times which causes us to think that the worship and love of God depends solely on how much we *feel* the right feelings, how much our consciousness is attuned to piety, how far we can be satisfied with our own state of mind.

All these worries and scruples attest, in fact, to the truth that

G

we are concentrating on *ourselves* rather than on our service. We find it hard to understand how an action, a gesture, a being together in a certain ritual attitude, can be effective, even though the political life of our times has shown only too clearly how effective political ritual, mass movement, national or party symbolism can be. We individualists despise these, and their strength has proved such as to make us rightly fear them. But if public ritual has a terrible power for destruction when abused by bad men, it also has a great potentiality for fuller life when properly used for the right end. It is so used in the liturgy, for in it we are taken out of ourselves in order to be the people of God, and, as we understand it all better, we are guided towards a more non-subjective type of private prayer in which, instead of over-worrying about ourselves, we are content to attend to God and let His will be done.

This, indeed, is essentially the theme of the wonderful prayers of the liturgy which are in sharp contrast with too many of the prayers of our devotional prayer-books.

I happen to be writing these lines on Ember Saturday in Lent, and I look up the collect of the day's Mass. It is one of the many acts of contrition which fill the liturgy: "Look favourably upon us, O God, our protector, so that we who are borne down by the weight of our sins may receive thy forgiveness and serve thee with untroubled minds." Note that while there is no attempt to suggest that we are better than we in fact know ourselves to be, "borne down by the weight of our sins", we are content with a humble and factual acknowledgement of the truth. The reality at once almost takes for granted God's forgiveness—"thy mercy having been received" in the Latin construction—and the climax of the prayer is that we should thus be enabled to serve God "with untroubled [Latin: 'free'] minds". That is what we need: to be in a state where we can carry out our life's meaning, the free service of God. The meaning of such a prayer suits equally the sinner and the saint, the Christian occupied with secular affairs and the Christian especially dedicated under rule to God's service.

In this, we see perhaps the greatest wonder of the liturgy, and the one that is almost relevant to the theme of these pages. It is for *all*, and each can take from it just what *he* most needs. Because it is primarily an *action* of worship and service, it makes the least demand of piety and personal devotion on those who just do not really feel pious and devout. Everyone can attend Mass—the unique commemoration of Calvary and the Resurrection. But not everyone wishes to do the Stations of the Cross, an infinitely lesser devotion. Yet do we not half-consciously think that the extra of the Stations some-how divides off the good from the only indifferent?

Because the liturgy enacts the Creation and the Incarnation within the cycle of the year and the cycle of the day, it auto-matically and eloquently relates the spiritual order to the tem-poral, and thus, even more for the laity perhaps than for the clergy or religious, it is a secular spirituality. The feasts of the year—holy days of obligation—and the Sunday when we com-memorate a kind of recurrent Easter, Christ's triumph at the root of our Christian faith, are attuned to the rhythm of life, and the addition of more frequent going to Mass on other feasts or daily, or the addition of the liturgical morning and evening prayer in Prime and Compline, fill out for those who want more and can profit from more the picture drawn in all its essential outlines by obligatory Mass.

Moreover, whatever practice we adopt, our liturgical life is united in the Church with the praise of the monks singing the Office in choir and the recitation obligatory for every priest. For it is the Church that is praying, and with which we unite ourselves in Christ's Mystical Body. Again, we see that every Mass, every liturgical prayer, in its beauty, simplicity and objectivity, equally serves the least religious as it serves the most religious. It is a prayer of honest sanity for the least devout; it is a mystical prayer for those who have more fully realized their relation to God.

And if, in fact, too few have come to realize how the liturgy (which for the priest and still more for the monk directly governs, and as it were encloses, their special and sacred mode of life) ministers to the spiritual needs of the very different life and vocation of the laity in the world, this is because so little has been done to introduce and explain its real meaning and function. But now much more is being done because we have become preoccupied again with the special problem of a secular spirituality no less important than, yet distinct from, the religious and clerical. In another chapter we can consider how the liturgy can be made the living centre of a true secular spirituality.

IX

THE LITURGY—SPIRITUAL CENTRE

I. THE LITURGY ALONE SURVIVES PERSECUTION

RECENTLY, I was talking to a very zealous and apostolic priest who has indeed been mainly responsible for organizing an important campaign for making the Church better known to the country. While fully agreeing about the great value of his work, I ventured to suggest that the real problem was one of getting Catholics to live lives whose essential Christianity would be the best witness of the Church in the world, and I referred to the importance of developing real living parishes and making the liturgy the centre of Christian spirituality and action. He smiled indulgently and said something about liturgical cranks. This, unfortunately, has been too common a view, and it is probably due in part to the attitude of would-be liturgical reformers, many of whom seem more interested in niceties of ritual and accuracy of chants. But since the Lugano Conference, held in September 1953, it can only be ignorance or bad-will which accounts for such a view of a movement enjoying the highest approbation of the Church and actively participated in by more and more clergy and laity of distinction and experience. At that conference, in which the Cardinal Archbishop of Genoa set the tone, it was the speech of the Bishop of Berlin which produced the greatest impression.

Bishop Weskamm spoke as a prelate whose spiritual authority lies in a land of persecution where his people are virtually deprived of all the aids to apostolic work which we enjoy in free countries. Religious education is at a minimum; press and publicity are openly hostile, and there are no means of any effective counter-action; Catholics themselves are suspect to the authorities if they are active Catholics, and their most innocent actions can be politically interpreted as hostile to country and régime.

What was the Church to do? "Our pastoral duty was clear. We had to make every effort to gather the individual faithful together and to incorporate them into the community of the Church. As in his natural life, so also as a Christian, man is fundamentally placed in a community: into the organism of the Church. Our task consisted therefore in gathering the many together, to awaken them spiritually, to bring them interiorly into contact with the life of the Church, and to build them into a congregation of Christ." In other words, forcibly deprived of all else, Catholics return to the *centre* which we are apt to neglect because of the profusion of secondary means. And what was the result? "Precisely as a result of our situation, we have also become aware as never before that there are numerous positive possibilities of parish community life and of Christian life as a whole that are inherent in the properly celebrated Sunday Mass." "The former, often thoughtless, churchgoing is superseded by a conscious coming together, inspired by the desire to become part of the assembly of God's people." And the bishop contrasts "the spirit of individualism", the "wish to be left alone", which are characteristic of "normal" parishes, with "the need to be together", when the faith itself is all that is left. When only the reality is left, the people gather for prayer; they gather to form a community; they gather in order to sing; and they gather to hear the Word of God. They find their home in the worship of God. Bishop Weskamm, from behind the Iron Curtain, can state in black and white something we rarely dare to say in freedom:

We should not allow ourselves to live under illusions. It is quite possible, for example, to get the faithful to receive Holy Communion frequently and also to go to Confession regularly, while at the same time unchristian conditions such as animosity, bickering in married life, etc., continue as before. *Religious practices do not necessarily affect efficaciously the lives of the faithful. . . . For the liturgy to be close to the people there must exist a living, spiritual contact between the liturgy and the people of God—and that means not only one or other particular group, but the general mass of the faithful.*

It is most interesting to see how the conditions of persecution have forced the Church back to that underlying reality which is so emphasized in the early Church—the community of the faithful which *is* the community of Christ. Liturgical reformers who are solely occupied with ritual and even those who are solely occupied with external reforms may well miss the heart of the matter, which is the realization of community in Christ.

Indeed, it is perfectly evident that in the conditions of the Church to-day only a small proportion of Catholics could ever regularly attend churches where the liturgy with all desirable reforms could possibly be carried out. Hard-working industrial and suburban churches, the lonely country mission, the motor-chapel, these are the foci of liturgy and worship in our days of what Bishop Weskamm has called in special relation to his own conditions, but which applies in a way to all, a Catholic *diaspora*. But so long as Catholics generally do not realize that their Christian dispersal into the world, if it is to be effectively Christian, depends on their gaining a sense of living religious community in Christ, even though the latter can only be visibly realized in the humblest way, the problem of secular spirituality will not be solved. Catholics, apart from minority exceptional types, will go on thinking that an automatic attendance at a church and the periodical individualist receiving of sacraments constitutes Christianity, even though this is virtually divorced from their life in the world, where they are indistinguishable from others. The parish, in other words, must become a living communion centred on the Mass.

2. THE MASS

To state the problem is far from being able to solve it in practice, but the great clue certainly lies in the liturgy itself which is a public action and a prayer of Christian fellowship.

Yet the Mass is usually celebrated in the manner least calculated to make this clear, while the preached Word of God is, as often as not, an exhortation to individualist piety joined with a moral homily. It would be foolish to deny that much of this is the result of circumstances. The priest may have to say two or even three Masses. He has to give catechetical instruction and evening services perhaps two or three times a week. The confessional may demand long hours, and he has the running of sodalities and confraternities and Catholic Action groups. He has hospitals and homes to visit. He must be ready to sign forms and witness documents. And, above all this, he has the financial administration of church and residence, and realizing that neither will survive without money, half his life is devoted to begging from the pulpit and elsewhere and organizing bazaars, raffles and pools. No wonder liturgy seems a luxury and the liturgical reformer a crank. And even if the occasional priest is determined to surmount these difficulties, no sooner has he begun to get his people accustomed to the deeper way of worship and prayer than he is replaced, perhaps, by a priest with totally opposite views.

Yet whatever the difficulties, they should not prove insurmountable in the end. The testimony of the Bishop of Berlin should stimulate consideration about priorities in the work of the priest. Is it more important to preoccupy oneself with many secondary devotions and societies, or to concentrate more on the primary? Could not the financial bogey be transferred to the faithful suitably organized to cope with it, thereby, as I have already suggested, adding to the reality of their sense of community through a common responsibility?

Meanwhile, however difficult the conditions, the Mass is said in every church, and it is from the Mass, with the sermon or instruction which is given during it, that the sense of Christian community develops. As Bishop Weskamm said, we are so imbued with the spirit of individualism that, as things are, we wish to be left alone. Our idea of the Mass is to pray it, or pray during it, in silence and, if possible, remote from the nearest worshipper. It is, we think, a business between God and ourselves.

But this is simply incorrect. In each Mass the whole Church is engaged since it is in virtue of Christ's promise to the Church and His delegated sacerdotal power to its priest that the celebrant acts and consecrates. In each Mass the whole Church offers through the priest and is offered in the persons of Christ's members. In each Mass those present not only make their own personal offerings with the priest, but they stand for the whole Church. Because of this, the people always have their part to play. Even if the server takes their spoken part, they still express their community outwardly in rising and kneeling together. In the Dialogue Mass or the people's sung Mass, the faithful once again take all or part of their spoken part. In Holy Week and on special occasions a procession of the people is integral to the ceremony, and a Communion procession exists in effect at many Masses where a large number of the faithful go to Communion. Pope Pius XII has recommended Communion at Mass from particles consecrated during that Mass so that in addition to the Communion procession there could well be a procession to bring up the symbolic offerings of bread and wine. The Communion itself is, above all, the common completion of the Sacrifice by the visible uniting of the faithful with Christ in His Eucharistic presence to form one unity with Him. The Christian community has united itself through the priest with Christ's sacrifice to the Eternal Father, and Christ gives Himself in return gift to the Christian community in the person of each of its members from the priest downwards.

So long as the Mass is said in a tongue now virtually unknown to the majority of the faithful, even the fullest ceremonial will scarcely establish the public and common nature of the rite. Following in a Missal translation, for those who can bother, is already at one remove from the public common act and a turning in on oneself. But this difficulty can be partly surmounted by the priest's instruction on the meaning and nature of the Mass. Should two priests be available, it can best be surmounted by one of the priests leading and explaining the people's part from the pulpit. But these are details which demand discussion and study in the light of the basic need, and the progress already made in bringing the Mass and the liturgy nearer to the people gives promise that far more may yet be done, even to the extent, in Cardinal Lercaro's words, of "the family of God in its liturgical assemblies" hearing "the word of God in its own mother tongue directly and immediately from the mouth of the minister".

But the point we are seeking to press here is that, in so far as the Mass and other liturgical ceremonies come to be seen and understood by the people as a common act of worship and service in which Christ, whose sacrifice and witness we share, grows within us as a Christian community and within us as individual persons, we in our turn become the better spiritually equipped, as Christians together and as Christian individuals, to live the Christian sacrificial life of witness which is our vocation in everything we do. It is not just a question of quantity, but of quality. The least naturally pious or devout derives his spiritual light and strength from the act of the liturgy in which he intelligently participates, just as the person far advanced in a mystical spirituality finds in this act of the liturgy a worship and service completely in tune with his personal self-dedication to God. Personal vocation and sanctification spring, as they should, from the Christian fellowship in Christ through the Church.

3. THE DIVINE OFFICE

Apart from the Mass and the administration of the sacraments, the Divine Office forms an essential part of the liturgy. In fact, for very many centuries it was considered the basis of the religious or monastic life, marking the phases of each day and night with the praise of God in common prayer and reading suited both to the cycle of the year and the time of the day. New Orders gave up the common recitation of the Office because of the active work they needed to perform in times and ways not easily to be fitted into a programme governed by that periodic prayer. As with secular priests, the recitation of the Office, though obligatory, was made in private at times that suited the day's active work. For the laity the public singing of Vespers and/or Compline, the Church's evening prayers, takes place, though only occasionally in this country, on Sundays.

The unpopularity of the Church's own evening service would seem to be due in part to the difficulty of popular participation in it without training the congregation, but it may be hazarded that the root of the trouble is that Vespers and Compline are recited in Latin, a fact that deprives them of very much meaning for most people. This is surely a pity for here again is a prayer that unites the congregation together, and unites it to the whole praise of God in the Church, a prayer, with its references to the yearly liturgical cycle and to the time of day, which, with its ceremonial and congregational part, is also a solemn action. In connection with this, a layman can only express wonder at the fact that in seminaries where the future priest is trained, the evening prayer in common is not Vespers, nor even Compline, but night prayers from modern manuals of devotion.

Meanwhile, not a few of the laity who have come to understand the significance of the liturgy are turning to the private recitation, in unity with the whole Church, of Prime as a morning prayer and Compline as an evening one. This fact is attested to by the demand for books which contain these two Hours. They can be conveniently printed because the changes in them from week to week are relatively small. Beyond this, there is an unsatisfied demand for volumes of Day Hours.

Perhaps this taste suggests the ideal of the "clericalized layman" or the formation of lay communities, reciting the Office and, living perhaps on the land, in partial segregation from the world. In so far as such devotion is thought of exclusively as an escape from the main field of Christian battle in our day, its motive could be thus interpreted. But it need not be. The Divine Office, though originally developed as the public prayer for those whose special ideal or office separated them from the world, adapts itself ideally in some of its shorter Hours for the layman who has found in the liturgy the real spiritual inspiration of his secular life. It is a prayer, when recited in a tongue fully understood, couched in that objective, God-regarding language that seems to me specially suitable for those whose lives make them shy of much of the sugary and hyperbolical language characteristic of so much modern devotion. Even those who appreciate such devotion for the wrong reasons may find a useful spiritual tonic in the more astringent and impersonal liturgical prayer of the Church. It is a matter of pride for us in England that the place of the Divine Office for secular spirituality has been for so many years symbolically upheld by its public singing every day in the first church of the land, Westminster Cathedral. If part of it at least could ever be sung there by the people themselves and in their mother-tongue, what a focus of secular spirituality it would be!

4. NEARER TO GOD

Let us bring these considerations to a close with a brief word about a point which I have already more than once hinted at. The layman, we have seen, while living, in his secular work, the praise and service of God in his priestly, teaching and ruling rôle in incorporation with Christ, needs, in varying measures according to his capacity, to be nourished and enlightened through regular religious observance, whose minimum quantity has been appointed by the Church. I have sought to show that the Church's liturgy centred in the Sacrifice of the Mass admirably fulfils precisely that requirement. But the liturgy, it seems to me, understood in the right way moves one towards something else, something which, for want of a better word, one has to call mystical or contemplative devotion. I have in another book discussed this subject at some length. It is sufficient here to suggest the close affinity between the objective, whole man, God-regarding prayer of the liturgy and the God-centred prayer that one must call mystical. The liturgy acts as a natural setting for the mystical type of prayer which specially fulfils the individual's relation to God within the fellowship of the Church. It is neither convenient nor easy for the layman, busied with perhaps an anxious and absorbing employment in the day and then returning home to a pleasant, but also absorbing, domestic life, to pop into a church or drop on his knees by his bedside, or even deliberately turn his thoughts to religious meditation or a form of prayer. Somehow, the two lives do not always fit properly together. The change from the secular to the devotional may well involve for many people a certain sense of artificiality, of forcing, of rather tiresome duty, not to speak of a certain self-consciousness which tends to make such piety self-regarding. The result may mean a giving up of the attempt altogether, or alternate periods of special devotion and special indifference to devotion.

But a quietly formed habit of what may be called attention to God, without words and even without thought, may very well balance the bending of energy and interest to secular occupations. God is seen here, not so much as a Person, not so much identified with Our Lord as a Man, but as a persisting spiritual dimension to life.

Just as we are aware of space and time, of the air we breathe, of beauty or ugliness surrounding us, without consciously adverting to them, so the proper spiritual observance and training can cause an habitual awareness of God without specifically making God the object of our consciousness. Instead God becomes rather the *subject* of our consciousness. Judgment, reflection, imagination cause us to isolate objects so that our consciousness can dwell on them. But behind this process there lies the self and all that goes to make it up. If God who is in the core of our self—that self of ours which lies deep behind the superficial selves we think of when we make ourselves the object of our thoughts—is allowed His real place in us, then we know all the time that He is in and around us without all the time consciously adverting to the fact. It is only necessary occasionally and without strain and fuss to remind ourselves of the fact.[1]

Liturgical prayer and action, by affecting not only our minds, but our whole being in itself and in relation to others, is a school

[1] A monk, writing recently to me, has stressed the value in this connection of St Thomas' "idea of knowledge by 'connaturality'. Because our nature is made in the image of God, when we learn to reflect on our nature and *know ourselves*, we come to know God personally and intimately as the one source and end of our being." In the life of grace we are in God's presence, as it were, through this inner realization of God, the object of our faith, as "connatural" with our being.

which can condition us to this habitual awareness of this all-important divine dimension of ourselves and of the world. And in so far as this happens, the occasional thought, the occasional prayer, comes naturally, not as a moral duty, but as the inevitable expression of the meaning which we know our life to have.

There is no Christian, however little of a "devout" person he may be, who cannot gently grow in this way into a God-awareness, and there is surely no way as clearly calculated as this to give meaning, direction and spiritual value to our most secular avocations. Thus they can become permeated with the qualities of dedication, charity, courage, understanding, purity, humility, truthfulness which mark the life of witness to Christ in the world—the life of the "alter Christus", whether it be lived in great things or small, whether it be but a distant and feeble imitation such as most of us weaker brethren are likely to have to be content with or the heroic, utterly self-abandoned imitation of the saint.

X

LAY SPIRITUALITY NOT A LUXURY

I. COMMON OBJECTIONS CONSIDERED

I HOPE I have succeeded in these pages in drawing some picture of an ideal of secular Christian spirituality, and of the rôle of the lay Catholic in the Church, faced as it is in these times with a world full of good, decent people caught up in the disorder of clashing ideologies and interests and carried along by the immense forces of a technological and impersonal age. It may be contended that what I have said bears in fact too little relation with secularist life and problems as they face the Christian. The intimate union of the Christian with Christ, with his sharing in Christ's priestly, prophetical and kingly powers, at bottom belongs to another world, a world that some would call "mystical" rather than real in the everyday sense of that word. It makes little visible difference, even though it may be of subjective importance and comfort. And when it comes to the liturgy, here again we are in another world of symbolism, beauty and instruction, but away from the hard realities of life as it has to be lived, by the Christian as much as by anyone else. More wearing and effective, surely, is the old tradition of hard, personal moral effort, with the clear sanctions of heaven or hell, and disciplined obedience and loyalty to the visible Church in the person of the priest and in the obligations of church attendance, or else . . . And those who want more, as they should, can find it in extra devotion and extra willingness to be a good parishioner and, if opportunity comes one's way, in being a good agent of Church policy in secular affairs.

The short answer to this, it seems to me, is that it simply is not working. And it will certainly be even less effective to-morrow than it is to-day. The leakage or drift away from the Church speaks for itself, even though exceptional conditions of disillusion in the world, coupled with the virtual collapse of so much non-Catholic Christianity, creates a good response to fresh methods of Catholic apostolate in the number of converts.

In Britain, it is enough to consider the number of Catholic immigrants, especially from Ireland, during more than a century, and, taking into account a natural birth-rate through that period, to calculate what the present size of the Catholic population should be, were it not for the immense defection. And, even working on the hopeful line of conversions, we are still forced to admit that, but for Catholic immigration, Catholic numbers to-day would be very small indeed. Yet, compared with the Continent and South America, the record in Anglo-Saxon Protestant countries is outstanding.[1]

But from the point of view of the theme of these pages, even more significant is the failure of Christians to be witnesses to Christ from within the world and, in consequence, to affect the world in itself. The common explanation for this is that Catholics are not sufficiently good Catholics. But is this a satisfactory explanation? In the first place, it suggests, under God, an unrealizable ideal. We have no reason to expect that the mass of Catholics will be "*devots*". The taste, the will, the character for a life either of marked piety and observance or of strong churchmanship are to be found in minorities, not majorities, of practising Catholics. But we must also have the courage to face the question as to whether the religiously fervent Catholic, the "good Catholic", is necessarily an effective witness to Christ in the world. Where he scores, if we may so put it, is in virtues which the world hardly understands and appreciates with difficulty. Regularity and even fervour in his religious life; a high standard of personal and family morality according to canons now widely thought to be too narrow and outdated; great loyalty to the visible, institutional Church and all that it obviously means—these in themselves are not neces-

---

[1] An American writer has put it thus: "Here are great masses of people held—and just barely held—to a decreasing minimum of religious duties by the back-breaking toil and nerve-wracking watchfulness of the clergy. We see people swarming down around that gridiron that holds them away from mortal sin, and constantly slipping through. We see earnest priests and sisters booting reluctant children along the road to salvation which they ought to run with joy. We see efforts made to render religion attractive, with Masses of short duration and at convenient hours and a laboriously worked out organizational and recreational programme to 'hold' the young people. And to persuade Christians to contribute enough money to finance the works of the Church, devices appropriate to Monte Carlo must be introduced. Atlas with straining muscles is holding up a globe, an inert mass. One must admire Atlas, and sympathize with him, and pray for him. But one must wonder why the mass is so heavy, considering that it is made up of redeemed men who have the divine life in them."—Willis D. Nutting in *Orate Fratres*, vol. xxiii, No. 2, p. 68.

sarily entirely impressive to others, and they are widely misunderstood. Still, if that were all, it would be of immense value.
There are very many who recognize and admire the faithful
Catholic with his doctrinal and moral certainties, his fidelity
and his loyalty. Unfortunately, however, all these are too
often not the whole story. With them can go a great deal of
shockingly unchristian behaviour and attitude of mind. The
self-centredness, lack of charity and sympathy, hardness,
pharisaism of the pious have almost become proverbial. But such
failings usually express themselves only in a narrow circle.
What is worse to-day is the public record. How often the
Christian sides with the oppressor against the oppressed, with
the intolerant against the tolerant. If there is a narrow, bitter,
reactionary, formalist party, it is likely to have Christian or
Catholic backers. Nationalism, militarism, the spirit of capitalism (whether in the possessing or in the trade union class)
find at least as much Christian support as secularist. If Catholics
are perhaps no worse than others for political and party
prejudice, uncouthly expressed, they are certainly no better.
Christian charity rarely penetrates those frontiers. Nor can one
fairly say that creative achievement, good taste, breadth of
soul and mind in using and expressing God's gifts to man
betoken the Christian—alas! it may well be the opposite.

It is true, thank God, that the too low standards of the
Christian and Catholic masses are often in keen contrast with
the heroism, devotion and charity of the few who really live
their faith, and perhaps nowhere are these to be found so fully
and consistently as in the Catholic orders devoted to the
works of mercy, to the sick, the poor, the unwanted.

But while, as I have said, it would be vain to expect a standard among Christians generally of those whom even the
world recognizes as saints—it was never so even in the days of
the first Christian enthusiasm, as the New Testament shows—
it is surely strange that there should be so little difference, to
put it as charitably as possible, between the Christian in his
daily worldly life and the non-Christian. Take away his
religious observance and his standards of personal and family
morality—no defence of birth-control and no divorce—and
how much difference is left? The difference, to say the least,
can be uncomfortably narrow.

Is it reasonable to expect very much more? some may ask.
The fundamental reason for these shortcomings lies, not in lack

of Christian virtue, but in lack of discernment, wisdom, education. Christianity does not provide intelligence and culture, nor can it alter stupidity and narrowness of character which may result from bad heredity, bad environment, lack of means and all kinds of extraneous reasons.

All this is certainly a large part of the explanation, but, in explaining, it also suggests how far we still are from enabling religion to play its part in compensating for such temporal defects. The tradition we live by is in fact derived from exceptional conditions—conditions which have been described as those of a state of siege. When the Church was thrown on the defensive through the rise of heresy, through violent anticlericalism and through the increasing popularity and power of a materialistic philosophy which seemed to promise a new world of discovery, progress and social happiness, the Church had first to safeguard doctrine, religious practice, personal devotion, extrinsic loyalties, all of which were visibly embedded in the institutional and external aspects of the Church. Simple conformity was the test, and it was all the more valuable in that it offered all that was essential and most precious in the Church: the Mass, the sacraments, prayer, the catechism, the rallying round the ordained priest, the divinely-made intermediary between Christ and man. Authority at a time when all authority was in question was safeguarded for millions. Moreover, the masses of the people were still uneducated and cut off from the books and other channels of thought and publicity that so definitely mark our own age. Thinking for oneself was largely out of the question, and new ideas were either authoritatively imposed or permeated down from powerful intellectual or social minorities. The Church's reaction and defence had to be of a kind appropriate to such conditions.

To-day, the situation is radically different. Religious, especially "Confessional", controversy is no longer in fashion; the philosophy of secularist progress is no longer in the ascendant; the masses are subject to a myriad self-contradicting influences which they can digest for themselves, even if they are far from being equipped to judge them intelligently. While there could never be any question of weakening doctrine and authority, of not insisting on the priorities of devotion, public and personal, of not encouraging proper loyalties, the question is whether these are sufficient by themselves to keep faithful large numbers of Catholics who could not, even if it were thought desirable, be safeguarded from secularist publicity, and to impress the millions to whom the "Church" is something alien and distant—of interest only to "special" people. It seems to me that only if Catholics generally can be got to see that Christianity is a life, a whole life in itself, will there be any chance of their living Christianity themselves and, in living it, spreading it around them.

Yet we cannot reckon on the mass of Catholics living what we call pious, devout or religious lives. The truly religious life is not, I venture to suggest, what we too often think it to be, namely a life of exceptional *religious* devotion and *personal moral* observance more or less detached from the indifferent and often evil ways of secular life; the truly religious life is the full spiritual flower of *the good life lived in the world and through the proper use of the things of the world*.

The universal Christian vocation is at the level where all can seriously try to live lives that habitually differ from secularist lives which are governed by self-regarding ambitions and appetites, while a minority will feel called and impelled to reach up nearer and nearer to God through a more perfect service from the common ground of basic Christian living.

Thus, it seems to me, we must honestly face the truth that a Catholic who fails in his secular life to manifest any of the fruits of the Holy Spirit is in fact a poor Christian, however regular his religious devotions and correct his keeping of the defined Christian law—whereas the Catholic who really tries to guide his life in the world by Christian principles of "love, joy, peace, patience, kindness, generosity, forbearance, gentleness, faith, courtesy, temperateness, purity", is a good Christian even if his religious and ecclesiastical "appurtenance" is and remains relatively small. In a way, this seems an obvious thing to say, yet the truth is far from apparent in Catholic training, education and instruction as these are too often given. These do not envisage a Christian way of life and living so much as the individual practice of detached Christian religious actions and the observance of certain moral rules abstracted from living as a whole.

This is perhaps inevitable, because instructions and sermons and observances and moral codes are themselves abstractions from living. To be effective, they *presuppose* a kind and quality of life lived, and it is with this life of Christian living that the fellowship of Catholics in Christ deals.

2. CHRIST-LIFE IN THE FELLOWSHIP OF THE CHURCH

Christ is the Way, the Truth and the *Life*—Christ, the Incarnate God, in the model of His own life on earth, and Christ, the Incarnate God, prolonging through His grace, which is His power and presence, His life in the Mystical Body which is the Church and in each of us as living members together of that Mystical Body. "I live now, not I, but Christ liveth in me." I have heard a very intelligent priest say that he thought this language was too remote and metaphorical to be of practical spiritual help. Yet surely it is the key to everything. Christ is alive—*the* Life, and our Christian life, our life, is His life in us through His grace. Though we have to play our part in co-operating with grace, we could not conceivably *live* Christianity, which is life at God's level, except through Christ's life. And life is not a thing which, as life, admits of degrees. You are alive or you are dead. Even if our life in and with Christ happens to be a poor and weak sort of life, it is still life, and life with Christ—a whole, living thing ever admitting of immense growth in all kinds of direction. Only mortal sin, by cutting off the channel of sanctifying grace, can temporarily deprive us of life with Christ, yet because of the permanent change in our spiritual constitution made by baptism, the flow of Christ's life into ours can be resumed by perfect repentance and sacramental confession.

Once we see all this we cannot properly think of Christianity and religion being, as it were, a half-dose of spirituality, as though we could fulfil our spiritual destiny in church and on Sundays or in merely external loyalties and observances. Strong or weak as our Christian life may be, it is a life, a whole, living thing, seeping into every recess of our being, whatever we may be doing. It is there sanctifying us (more or less, according to our co-operation, our will, our understanding and appreciation) in all we do with a right intention, whether in church or out of it, whether on Sundays or weekdays. And, looking at it the other way round, our failure to understand, to be inspired, to co-operate, is just as much of a tragic loss if it occurs in our secular life as in our specifically religious. But, while we always need the renewal of spiritual vigour which pours into us from Mass and the sacraments, from prayer and devotion, from observance and loyalty to the Church which is Christ, we shall no longer think of these as externally derived additions to an artificial Christian construction; we shall think of them as we think of the food which keeps our bodily lives healthy and strong. Food, to do its work, presupposes a healthy whole, a good life. Our Lord Himself not only chose the analogy of food for our souls, but literally gave Himself in His Eucharistic presence as the food of our spiritual life and our mode of "communion" in His sacrifice to the Godhead. Health, balance, wholeness, integrity, these are just as much the qualities of the Christian spiritual life as they are of our material life—and religious indigestion can be as harmful as bodily indigestion.

"While there's life, there's hope" is an old proverb. It is very applicable to the spiritual situation. When we realize that our Christianity is our life, we realize that there is always spiritual hope. We may be weak and sinful, by nature disinterested in religion as such and intensely interested in ourselves and our ambitions, but we, with all our feebleness and selfishness, know ourselves to be spiritually alive, to have Christ, so that a fuller, a more abundant Christian living is always in potential development.

Everyone understands the meaning and attraction of phrases like "living more fully", "developing our personalities", "getting more out of life". These are constructive, hopeful phrases which suggest the expansion of what we already know to be within ourselves. They lie at the base of good education. When we understand that they are as true—indeed much truer—of the spiritual life, we shall begin to lose the very real fear of "being good", of belonging to the minority of the "devout-minded", of being somehow in a religious class apart from others. Much of this fear, indeed, is due to the way in which religious goodness has been misunderstood to mean precisely the lack of balance, the artificiality, the smugness, of a piety that is plastered on from without rather than grown from within in a living, balanced whole. The formal realization of how each of us in his life as a Christian becomes "another Christ" in exercising within the Church the priestly, prophetical and kingly functions of Christ, will not of course automatically lead to a well-rounded, good, Christian life, of apostolic value; but the gradual realization of what this really means in the way of vocation, human dignity, meaning and purpose in life cannot but be an extremely powerful motive in life for living, in all things, worthy of the fruits and promise of the Redemption.

And if one fails, as fail more or less one will, how close and powerful is the motive for looking again to Our Lord for the life He wants to share with all, sinners no less than saints.

But, as I have insisted, all this is not a mere question of individuals seeking their own personal salvation. It is not enough to think of human life as a kind of individual trial to see if we can make the spiritual grade. To think of it that way is, consciously or unconsciously, to sacrifice others for our personal spiritual benefit, and thus surely to weaken our own spiritual growth. We have seen how Christ's sacrifice as a perfect High Priest was to reconcile mankind to God and create the conditions within which Christ's Kingdom can be built up even in this valley of exile—the Kingdom which will be realized when Christ comes again to make His final public judgment of good and bad, right and wrong, death and life. To ensure this He founded the Church and in it prolonged His own constant mystical presence in the world. That Church infallibly and authoritatively preserves His "Good News" and keeps open the visible channels of His Grace (which is His life in us) as He willed them to be. But that Church lives in the unity and fellowship of its members who are the cells of the Mystical Body of which Christ is the Head. This fellowship, this community, is all-important, for it is in fact the Church living in the world and witnessing to Christ. The authority, the order, the material churches, the schools, these are the means, directly or indirectly instituted by Christ and willed by Him, necessary for preserving the conditions of the Christ-life of the Church as a whole in the Christ-life of each member. We are individual, because our final end as creatures stamped with God's own image is a personal fulfilment in the Beatific Vision; but we are also a unity together, a fellowship, because it is the Church—Christ in the Church—which is the living witness of God's truth under the inspiration of the Holy Spirit.

This fact has a particular relevance in these days when men are bound together in the different societies through which their secular ends are protected and furthered. We may rightly judge that the true good of the person has often been sacrificed to the end of State and society in the modern world. But this does not take away from the fact that man has grown more and more accustomed to think and act in terms of social units rather than in terms of individual initiative and effort. There is certainly no call to underrate the vast importance of individual

work and example in the Church. The record of the saints and
holy men and women through the ages is there to remind us of
the truth. But the Church, unlike human societies, perfectly
links the individual with the whole and the whole with the
individual. The saint springs from the fellowship of the Church
—consider the history of the great religious orders—and the
fellowship of the Church is the school for saints. Both aspects
must be kept in balance. Unfortunately, conditions of social
life have made it difficult in most ages to realize the fellowship
of the Church whose final form will be the full Communion of
the Saints. A religious order and even the clergy as a whole
make a visible fellowship because they are in fact separated
from the world. But the fellowship of all Christians, the fellowship of the Church itself, flows in an indistinct and undefined
way through the world when it is viewed phenomenally. Yet it
is absolutely real, and the more we can come to realize it, the
more effective will be the witness of the Church, especially in
our times, and the more we ourselves will be helped in living our
own spiritual lives. We cannot however take a short-cut in order
the better to realize it. The clergy and religious orders have
specific rôles and dignities within the Church, and consequently
their social life is in part cut off from the world. But the
faithful as a whole cannot take a short-cut to pseudo-Church-
manship without running the risk of living double lives. We
belong to the world, every human being of which Christ came
to save and every piece of which has its place in Christ's
Kingdom. We have therefore to find and express our fellowship
in Christ within the world and its temporal life. And this is all
the more important in that God alone knows the final reckoning
of those who are at heart with Christ and those who are against
Him. Nor can we doubt that one great test will be "which was
our neighbour?"

The more we can realize that we belong to one another in
Christ and the more we are encouraged to see this in parish,
diocese, country, world, not so much in formally religious
gatherings and actions, but in the free, conscientious carrying
out of our secular functions, the fuller will be our new Christian
lives and the stronger the power of Christianity in the world.
Indeed, it is impossible to doubt that a sense of Christian
fellowship growing from the common Christian values and
standards of more and more balanced, integrated Catholics
would have a revolutionary effect on the world. Catholics will

differ in many ways, in secular loyalties, in interests, in political views, but such differences of natures, vocations and means to the end are compatible with profounder unities of standards, conduct, principles, values, ends, and they can be seen by the world to be so compatible. It has been a noticeable feature of our times that the growth of secularism and paganism has inevitably narrowed the differences between serious Christians. Even so the true sense of fellowship cannot be imposed; it must spring from below and within. It must be the result of free, responsible Christian lives. Men think for themselves to-day— or think they think for themselves. It is for us truly *to think for ourselves* within the Faith and Revelation of the Christ whose life is within us. There is no alternative in the civilized world as it is constituted to-day.

I have tried to show how the centring of our lives in the life of Christ, incarnated on earth and in the Church which is His Mystical Body of which each of us personally shares the Christ-life, unfolds a pattern of secular Christian living to which one cannot really apply the most abused words of "piety", "devoutness", "churchiness"—words derived from a conscious or unconscious separation of the Church (which is Christ) from the world (which is also Christ in its Christian members). This secular Christian living, within the Church as the visible, God-founded institution and as the equally God-founded fellowship of its members, is a *life*—the Christ-life in our life—and, as a life, susceptible of growth, balance, integrity, realization, value, end (or the opposites) rather than of marks that can be numerically tabulated and differentiated. Devotion, piety, religious observance, saying prayers, external loyalties —at all stages these are necessary for our spiritual invigoration and direction, but they only flower in their true fullness and beauty when they become the inevitable expression of the ever closer realization of the divine which marks the fuller growth of the Christian life.

And because to the spiritual Christ-life of the individuals and of individuals together in the fellowship of the Church corresponds the story of our human history, the rhythms and cycles of the seasons and the days, and, above all, the living epic of our salvation achieved by the Incarnate God in His supremely pleasing and victorious Sacrifice, I have suggested that the natural prayer and service to God must be, pre-eminently, the public, social prayer of the Church: the liturgy.

That prayer frames the central and unique act of worship, the Sacrifice of the Mass, which joins the offering of the whole Christian body, the Church, and the offering of ourselves, to Christ's perfect offering and "at-one-ment" to God, and makes the communion of each of us with Christ in His Eucharistic presence, as confirming the wonder of the sacrifice. It is a prayer of subjective and objective perfection, in its prodigality of Christian teaching which parallels the phases and trials of secular Christian life. In it there is no call for artificial emotional feelings, no danger of introversion, no excuse for hypocrisy and the "holier than others" attitude which so easily underlies even protests of abject humility. Together, in a common action of common prayer, we speak with mind and body to God, and to the Blessed Virgin and the Saints who carry our prayers on high that our personal Christian life and the Christian life of us all in the Church which is Christ's Mystical Body may attain the supreme purpose and end in the personal vision of God in the timeless Communion of Saints. Thus our life can "be inspired, as His glorious power can inspire you, with full strength to be patient and endure: to endure joyfully, thanking God our Father for making us fit to share the light which the saints inherit, for rescuing us from the power of darkness, and transferring us to the kingdom of His beloved Son".[1]

That strength to be patient; to endure joyfully; to be made fit to share the light which the saints inherit; to be rescued from the powers of darkness; and finally to attain the Kingdom— that strength is acquired by living our daily lives in and with Christ. We, the lay people of His Mystical Body, His Fellowship, share His priesthood in our sacrifices, sufferings, choices, which under the guidance of the Holy Spirit are made by Him acceptable to the Holy Trinity. We share His teaching authority by witnessing by our actions, our speech, our thoughts to the way He told us to live in love of God and our neighbours. We share His Kingship by trying to be "other Christs" in carrying out His plan to achieve the Kingdom whose triumph He will proclaim on the Last Day. And it is from Him alone that we, with our sinfulness and stupidity, can derive the spiritual power to fulfil this priestly, prophetical and royal responsibility, within His Revelation, for the peace and happiness of mankind on earth and its glory with God for eternity.

[1] Colossians I. 11–13.